Robert A. Ullrich is professor of management and associate dean, the Owen Graduate School of Management, Vanderbilt University, Nashville, Tennessee.

Motivation Methods That Work

Robert A. Ullrich

A SPECTRUM BOOK

Prentice-Hall, Inc., Englewood Cliffs, New Jersey 07632

Library of Congress Cataloging in Publication Data

Ullrich, Robert A.
   Motivation methods that work.

   (A Spectrum Book)
   Bibliography: p.
   Includes index.
   1. Employee motivation.   2. Personnel management.
   I. Title.
   HF5549.5.M63U44   658.3′14   81-10549

ISBN 0-13-603860-3

ISBN 0-13-603852-2 {PBK.}

This Spectrum Book is available to businesses and organizations
at a special discount when ordered in large quantities.
For information, contact Prentice-Hall, Inc., General Book Marketing,
Special Sales Division, Englewood Cliffs, N. J. 07632.

© 1981 by Prentice-Hall, Inc., Englewood Cliffs, New Jersey 07632

A SPECTRUM BOOK

10 9 8 7 6 5 4 3 2 1

Printed in the United States of America

Editorial/production supervision by Shirley Covington
Cover design by Tony Ferrara Studios, Inc.
Manufacturing buyer: Cathie Lenard

Prentice-Hall International, Inc., *London*
Prentice-Hall of Australia Pty. Limited, *Sydney*
Prentice-Hall of Canada, Ltd., *Toronto*
Prentice-Hall of India Private Limited, *New Delhi*
Prentice-Hall of Japan, Inc., *Tokyo*
Prentice-Hall of Southeast Asia Pte. Ltd., *Singapore*
Whitehall Brooks Limited, *Wellington, New Zealand*

For My Parents

Marie M. Ullrich
and the late
Albert H. Ullrich

Contents

Preface

This is a book for managers. My purpose in writing it is to demonstrate a number of techniques that can be used in organizations to alleviate serious situations such as declining labor productivity and increasing rates of absenteeism. The problem is that relatively few organizations have taken advantage of these techniques.

I have selected some of the oldest techniques, rather than the newest ones, to illustrate the nature of this problem. The techniques described are not recent fads: Their usefulness has been demonstrated time and again by scientists and managers alike. Yet, as I have said, relatively few organizations have attempted to benefit from them.

None of the techniques is complicated. Managers do not need a string of higher degrees to implement them. All that may be needed is an incentive to use them, which this book attempts to provide.

Data appearing in Tables 1-1, 1-2, and 1-3, and in parts of the text are from Kim and Hamner. © 1976 American Psychological Association. They are reprinted by permission.

Introduction

The facts are clear enough: Between 1947 and 1966 labor productivity in this country increased each year by an average of 3.2 per cent. Then, the rate of growth started to decline, and from 1966 to 1973 productivity increases averaged 2.1 per cent. The next six-year period saw the annual growth in labor productivity fall off to an average of 0.8 per cent.

Although the problem may seem clear, its causes appear to be so numerous and profound that the average manager may despair of reversing the trend. Worker alienation, government regulation, high interest rates, energy shortages, and a multitude of other factors in the economy interact to depress productivity—and we see the effects in our offices and factories.

Ironically, there is much that can be done in the factory and office to increase the productivity of employees. Furthermore, there are numerous improvements that the average manager or supervisor can make without investing in additional equipment or employing expensive consultants. Managers very much like you have used a variety of relatively simple techniques to increase the quality and quantity of employee productivity and to decrease absenteeism, turnover, and grievances. They have accomplished these goals with a variety of occupational groups, ranging from research and development personnel at one extreme to unskilled laborers at the other.

From the experience of these managers, as well as from the scientific work in this field, four major points emerge. These points are the themes that organize this book:

1. *What works in one occupation or setting will not necessarily work in all others.* Management's actions must be tailored to fit the work environment.

2. *What works in theory generally works in practice.* The implication is that one cannot expect to modify practice successfully without understanding the theory on which it is based.

3. *What works needs to be worked at.* Without management of one form or another, organizations become disorganized.

4. *What works over the long run is structure.* Even spectacularly successful programs tend toward dissolution when their originators leave unless the programs are incorporated into the organization's structure. By structure, I mean policies, rules, procedures, and hierarchies of authority as well as norms, understandings, tacit agreements, and the like.

These four points are explained in detail later on. For now, it is important to add a fifth point and to dwell on it briefly:

5. *It is not unusual for problems to persist even though potential solutions are at hand.*

A number of examples of this come to mind, but my favorite was described by Frederick Winslow Taylor, the "father of scientific management." In 1911 Taylor reported some of his early attempts to increase labor productivity. One such attempt dealt with improving the productivity of skilled machinists. Taylor found that a 40 per cent gain in productivity could be achieved merely by directing a stream of cooling water at the spot where the machinist's tool was removing metal from the part being made. The water carried away heat generated in the process of cutting metal. As a result, the cutting process could be speeded up without burning the cutting tool. Prior to Taylor's discovery, cutting speeds were limited by the amount of heat generated and by the melting point of the cutting tool.

To take advantage of the 40 per cent gain in productivity that Taylor had made possible, the company that supported Taylor's work built a new machine shop equipped with water pipes leading to each machine tool, water drains, pumps, storage tanks, and the like. Moreover, the firm invited its competitors to visit the shop to learn how a simple change could yield a 40 per cent increase in cutting speed. But in 20 years, Taylor said only one competitor took advantage of his discovery, and he was a former employee who actually had worked with Taylor's innovation.

It does not seem possible that intelligent managers would have ignored a simple technique that had been demonstrated beyond doubt to be profitable. Yet this is not unusual. In fact, all the techniques discussed in the following chapters have been available for years. They have been used successfully in a variety of organizations, and they are described in great detail in the management literature. You probably have read or heard about most of them but have not attempted to use any of them in your own organization.

Part of management's reluctance to adopt new ways of managing work, even when those ways have been demonstrated to improve productivity, is attributable to the way in which these techniques have been advocated. Typically, advocates favor a single approach and, unknowingly, exaggerate its applicability in organizations. Furthermore, although most of us have heard through the grapevine how the XYZ Company chalked up a spectacular flop using one technique or another, the advocates of such techniques have not been particularly critical in describing the limits and "fragility" of their approaches. Any endeavor can be botched—particularly when we are uninformed about the limits of what we are trying to do. Finally, managers have been led to assume that useful techniques cannot be implemented without the help of expensive consultants. Concern for costs is understandable, but the costs in this case are not inevitable.

The other part of the problem is yours. All of us are uncomfortable when it comes to changing familiar ways of doing things. Within limits, though, such discomfort is natural and quite necessary in organizations. Although I cannot do much to ease the discomfort that accompanies change, I will try to convince you of its inevitability.

One of the most frustrating aspects of organizational life is a pervasive form of conservatism that makes time-honored but demonstrably inadequate practices seem preferable to untried solutions to problems. Such frustration led an anonymous wag to propose what are now called The Laws of Organizational Change. The First Law states that things that do not change remain the same. The Second Law, which follows logically from the First Law, states that if you do not want things to remain the same, you must change something. According to the Third Law of Organizational Change, things that change are no longer the same.

There is the truth in jest. The means to improve worker productivity are available, and they can be applied successfully to a broad spectrum of jobs. I hope to convince you that these means are at your disposal and that the potential for gain is worth the discomfort of changing some time-honored but inadequate ways of managing work.

To do this, I begin with a chapter on one of the simplest methods available. I use case histories as well as empirical data on the techniques' costs and results to introduce the method in question. Next, I explain the theory on which the technique is based. Finally, I elaborate on procedures and caveats. This format is followed in all the remaining chapters with the exception of the second and the last. The second chapter acknowledges the fact that what works in one setting will not necessarily work in all others. Reasons for this are explained, and a method of selecting techniques that fit a particular work setting is provided. The last chapter looks at ways of using experts, because some ways are better than others. As I have said, although it is not essential to use consultants, you may want to nonetheless. Thus, we look at the kinds of help that are available and some productive ways of using such help. Finally, each remaining chapter explains and illustrates techniques that can be used to manage workers at progressively higher levels in the organization.

For the moment, though, we turn to the problem of improving productivity among unskilled, relatively uneducated workers who have little, if any, commitment to their organization. For a long time, managers despaired of ever being able to solve this sort of problem. As it turns out, it may be one of the easiest to solve.

1

Alienated
Workers

ALIENATION

It is 2:00 P.M. on the first Saturday after Christmas. I have at least three hours in which to write, and I am grateful that it is Saturday and that I will not be interrupted today. I like to write. In fact, a great deal of what I do for a living is as enjoyable and as important to me as my leisure activities are. Apparently, Douglas McGregor was right: "Work *is* as natural as play or rest." [Emphasis mine.]

Unfortunately, many people have jobs in which they take little pride or pleasure. They are alienated from work because they find it lacks value and meaning. The further down we look in the organization's hierarchy of authority, the more numerous such people become.

The reason for this seems fairly straightforward. At the lowest occupational level, jobs tend to be simple, repetitive, and extraordinarily dull. People employed in such jobs tend to have few occupational skills, but their jobs require even fewer. Children could perform adequately many of the tasks to which adult lives are devoted. Clearly, such labor cannot compete effectively with leisure activities for the worker's interest.

It would be incorrect, though, to conclude that alienated workers are the inevitable products of monotonous jobs, for this conclusion would rest on the preposterous assumption that ambitious, energetic young adults can be transformed into alienated, unmotivated workers by a few months' employment in an office or factory. A more plausible assumption is that prior to entering the labor force, many of these workers were exposed to 18 to 20 years of experiences that alienated them from the traditional American belief in the dignity and value of work.

Regardless of who is to blame for their plight, these workers appear to be trapped in situations from which they cannot extricate themselves. They tend to dislike their jobs; yet they cannot escape them. The success story of advancement to management from humble beginnings on the shop floor is a folk tale from another era, and these workers know it. Given their general level of education relative to what is required of management recruits, the shop floor workers' prospects for advancement—for careers—are bleak.

Opportunities in other organizations are equally scarce for these workers. Again, given their work experience and education, quitting the company to find better jobs often results in employment at tasks that are no better than the ones at which they last worked. They know this, too, or they learn it after changing jobs a few times. So it goes.

The result is an all too familiar problem—workers who, at best, are indifferent about their work. They will work hard enough to keep their jobs, but not much harder. They will do enough to keep their supervisors off their backs, but not much more. They would prefer not to work at all, and they use their sick leave for unofficial holidays whenever they can. If their performance is to be maintained at an adequate level, their work must be checked regularly and their activities monitored frequently by various control procedures that are costly to maintain.

When you meet an employee who fits this description, you should say to yourself, "I wish I had six employees just like this one." The reason you should say this is that you probably have dozens of alienated employees, and you would be far better off if you only had six.

IMPROVING THE PRODUCTIVITY
OF UNSKILLED, ALIENATED WORKERS

The Preliminaries

Many people despair of improving the productivity of workers who care little for their jobs or for the organizations that employ them, but some firms have found a simple technique to be effective in accomplishing this. What follows is the story of how one company put the technique to work. Please bear in mind that although the workers in this example are unskilled, they are not necessarily alienated to the extreme degree depicted in the foregoing stereotype. Alienation is a matter of degree. Yet, for reasons to be explained later, this technique seems particularly appropriate for dealing with relatively unskilled employees—particularly those who are alienated from their jobs.

Several years ago, management in one of the Bell System plants participated in an experiment designed to compare the effectiveness of various techniques for improving worker productivity.[1] One of the more successful techniques was used with a group of janitors.

Management wanted to improve four dimensions of the janitors' performance: (1) cost, (2) absenteeism, (3) safety, and (4) service (that is, the quality of work performed). For a start, measures of these four dimensions of performance were obtained. As we shall see, this is a critical part of the technique, for it provides a basis for establishing concrete goals for employees as well as a format for feedback on their subsequent performance.

[1] J. S. Kim and W. C. Hammer, "Effect of Performance Feedback and Goalsetting on Productivity and Satisfaction in an Organizational Setting," *Journal of Applied Psychology*, 61 (1976), 48–57.

As it turned out, measures of performance were already used by the accounting department and were readily adapted for management's purposes. However, similar measures are simple enough to develop, and the lack of existing measures should not deter you from using the technique.

The measure of cost used was the ratio of standard to actual costs. From historical data, the company had developed standard cost estimates for each of the janitorial services performed. To evaluate the cost of actual service, management merely compared actual costs for these services with the standard estimated costs.

Absenteeism was still easier to measure, for it was defined as the percentage of shifts an employee failed to work over a given period of time. Five absences over a period of 100 shifts, for example, constituted an absenteeism rate of 5 per cent.

An employee's safety record was calculated by assigning increasing point values to accidents of increasing severity. For example, a personal injury accident resulting in lost time would carry more points than an accident resulting in a superficial injury. A perfect safety record was worth 100 points, and the point value of each accident was subtracted from each employee's score for the period.

Perhaps the most difficult dimension of work to measure was the quality of service. Yet an adequate measure was devised. Different parts of an employee's job were assigned different point values. For example, clean floors were assigned a higher point value than clean walls, presumably because floors need more frequent cleaning than walls. Supervisors rated each aspect of an employee's work according to this system and totaled the employee's scores. Flawless performance in all aspects of an employee's job was worth a total of 100 points.

The next step was to establish goals for employee performance. As shown in Table 1–1, the goal for cost was a ratio of 0.98. That is, actual costs were not to exceed standard cost estimates by more than approximately 2 per cent. This may seem to be a rather conservative goal for management to have set, but this was not the case at all, as we shall see.

Table 1–1
Performance Measures and Goals

Target	Performance Measures	Goals
1. Cost	$\dfrac{\text{Standard Cost Estimate}}{\text{Actual Cost}}$	0.98
2. Absenteeism	Percentage of Shifts Absent	4.7
3. Safety	100 (Point Score for Accident)	87
4. Service	Supervisor's Ranking of Work on a 100-Point Scale	83

The second goal was to limit absenteeism to the average rate prevailing in the area, which was found to be 4.7 per cent. The goal for safety was set at 87 points. This is a difficult kind of objective to establish, as is the goal for absenteeism. Achieving perfect safety or absenteeism scores may do more harm than good in the long run. Workers who are committed to achieving such goals have been known to cover up accidents and to report to work even when they were ill. Such dedication is misplaced, for it is neither in the employee's interest nor the company's to have the ill and the injured untreated and at work. Thus, a safety goal, such as the 87 points used in this example, must be set high enough to encourage a reduction in accidents, but not so high that it discourages employees from reporting the accidents that to some extent are inevitable.

Having established these four goals, management began to collect what are called *baseline data*—that is, data on actual, day-to-day accomplishments on the four performance dimensions. These data were to be used in evaluating each employee's progress in attaining the goals established by management.

The baseline observations, summarized in Table 1–2, indicated that actual costs were exceeding standard costs—the ratio of standard to actual costs was found to average 0.72. Clearly, a margin for improvement existed.

Room for improvement was less evident in the case of absenteeism, though, for the baseline observations indicated an average absenteeism rate of only 2.92 per cent—a rate

Table 1–2
Performance Goals vs. Actual Performance

Target	Actual	Goal
Cost	0.72	0.98
Absenteeism	2.92%	4.7%
Safety	76.98	87
Service	76.13	83

considerably below the geographic area's average absenteeism rate of 4.7 per cent. Given the preceding observations on the inadvisability of setting excessively stringent absenteeism goals, it is not clear whether an improvement in attendance should have been anticipated. In any event, it should be evident that goal setting ought to follow the collection and evaluation of baseline data, rather than precede these activities, as was the case in the present example.

According to the company's calculations, their employees' safety record was good for a C+. The employees scored an average of 76.98 points out of a possible 100. The goal of 87 points, once attained, obviously would serve the employees' and the company's best interests.

Finally, service also was found to be in the C+ range. The average evaluation of work was 76.13 points out of 100. To continue the analogy, the goal of 83 points constituted a respectable grade of B.

The Technique of Goal Setting

By this point, the company had accomplished some important tasks that often are omitted in less successful change programs. First, collecting baseline data resulted in fairly accurate descriptions of employee performance in the areas of interest to management. Second, management was able to establish measurable performance goals. More important, though, was management's success in defining problems in a way that permitted them to be solved. You see, if we define a productivity problem such as this one to be the result of poor worker attitudes, or a lack of motivation, or poor communication, we are likely to lose sight of our goal, which is to improve productivity. We are likely to become distracted by the problem of changing attitudes or improving communications. Granted, these are worthwhile endeavors for management—and should be attempted in any case. However, the relationship between attitudes and productivity is only hypothetical in this example, and we may find that improved attitudes do not inevitably result in improved productivity. In the present example, management defined the problem to be changing the cost ratio from 0.72 to 0.98, the safety score from 76.98 to 87, and so on. Thus, attention was directed toward attaining the desired outcomes rather than altering hypothetical constructs such as attitudes.

What management did at this point sounds simple, and it is. On Monday, supervisors met with their subordinates to set performance goals in each of the four areas where improvements were to be sought. Then, on Friday, the workers filled out evaluation forms on which they rated their own performance in each of the areas. They had been trained to make the same kinds of performance evaluations their supervisors made of their work. On the basis of these self-evaluations and similar ratings made by supervisors during the week, the supervisors reviewed performance relative to the week's objectives and praised workers whose performance had improved over that of the prior week or had exceeded the week's goals. Similar praise was given throughout the week as the supervisors' routine evaluations of their employees' work indicated that performance had been improved or that goals were being met and exceeded. On the next Monday, the cycle was begun again, as supervisors met with their subordinates to establish new goals in light of the prior week's achievements.

It is important to note that employees were not criticized or otherwise punished when their performance failed to improve or to surpass the goals set by management. They merely were reminded of the goals and helped and encouraged to meet them. As you know, behavior of this sort is far easier to describe than to enact. We are accustomed to criticizing others for unsatisfactory performance and to using threats of punishment to get others to behave as we want them. Such behavior on the part of supervision would not have improved productivity, and it might have detracted from management's success.

Table 1–3
The Results

Target	Baseline	30 Days	60 Days	90 Days	Goal
Cost	0.72	1.29	0.84	1.08	0.98
Absenteeism	2.92%	(no significant change)			4.7%
Safety	76.98	86.86	90.33	94.16	87.0
Service	76.13	82.34	83.83	83.67	83.0

And what was management's success? Table 1–3 tells the story. After three months, the cost ratio had increased to 1.08, surpassing the goal of 0.98 established by management. Absenteeism remained lower than the industry average in the area, and it did not change significantly. Safety improved; by the end of the 90-day period, the janitors' safety score reached 94.16, surpassing the initial goal of 87, and representing a substantial improvement over the baseline score of 76.98. Finally, service was rated at 83.67 by the end of the period—up from 76.13 at the beginning and edging past the goal of 83.

How Goal Setting Works

By now, you may have realized that the technique employed in the Bell System plant is an adaptation of B. F. Skinner's positive reinforcement. Positive reinforcement is nothing more than applied learning theory. It is simple to explain. *Most behavior is learned.* Infants are not programmed at birth to become lazy or ambitious, honest or deceitful, and happy or melancholy as adults. Rather, in Skinner's words: ". . . men are made good or bad and wise or foolish by the environment in which they grow."[2] *Most learning results from rein-*

[2] B. F. Skinner, *Walden Two*. Toronto: Macmillan, 1970, p. 273.

forcement. People learn to repeat behaviors that are rewarding; that is, rewards reinforce the behavior on which such rewards depend.

Praise is rewarding for most people. I am convinced that the average worker feels that management does not adequately recognize good work. In any event, positive reinforcement theory tells us that people are likely to repeat behaviors that are rewarded. Thus, the employee who is praised for having an improved safety record—for having avoided accidents—is likely to continue avoiding accidents. It's as simple as that.

To change employee behavior, management must precisely define and control the factors that control such behavior. As we saw in the Bell System example, this is accomplished in the four steps that are summarized in Figure 1–1. First, we must define desired behavior or goals in a way that permits them to be measured. The rationale for this is quite simple. If you cannot measure performance, you cannot tell when performance has been improved.

Figure 1–1

Using Positive Reinforcement

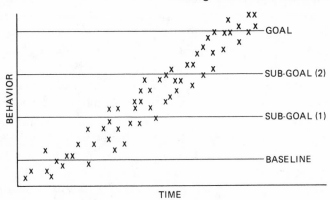

1. DEFINE DESIRED BEHAVIORS OR GOALS IN A WAY THAT PERMITS THEM TO BE MEASURED.
2. COLLECT BASELINE DATA ON PRESENT BEHAVIOR.
3. SELECT A LEVEL OF BEHAVIOR TO BE REWARDED AND THE FREQUENCY OF OCCURRENCE OF BEHAVIOR THAT MUST BE OBTAINED BEFORE MOVING TO A HIGHER GOAL.
4. DETERMINE THE NATURE AND FREQUENCY OF REWARDS TO BE USED.

The next step is to collect baseline data on the activities that are to be improved. Again, it is unreasonable to expect to be able to improve performance without first having measured the level of performance to be improved.

Following this, goals and subgoals are established. Because it is not always reasonable to expect that goals can be met immediately, it is often useful to approach goals in stages by setting successively higher subgoals and moving them from one to the next as each is achieved. However, this raises the question: What constitutes goal attainment? Should we move on to the next subgoal the day after, the week after, or the month after the present one has been met? The answer depends on the situation, and a general answer is not possible. However, it is better to wait a while to let newly learned behavior become habitual than it is to move to a higher goal prematurely. A little common sense goes a long way at this point.

Finally, one must determine the nature of the rewards to be used and the frequency with which desired behavior is to be rewarded. Typically, praise is given as a reward; it costs nothing and most people seem to like it. In theory, you can use anything, so long as people find it rewarding. However, a brief look at a few of the unanticipated problems encountered in using rewards is instructive.

One company tried using a six-pack of beer as a reward for improved performance. However, the workers who did not like beer did not view a six-pack as a meaningful reward, and the teetotalers thought that the whole thing was the work of the devil. Another firm used money to reward employees who achieved attendance goals. Their supervisors objected, though, on the grounds that it is immoral to pay people merely for showing up on time for work. After all, no one paid the supervisors for merely coming to work. In this case, management discontinued the program even though it was less costly to reward good attendance than it was to operate with the higher rates of absenteeism and tardiness that existed before the program was started. From these examples you can see the kinds of problems you can get into inadvertently if the technique is not thought out carefully.

Deciding on the frequency with which rewards are to be given constitutes another problem but one that has less dramatic potential consequences. Again, should we reinforce desired behavior each time it occurs, or weekly, or randomly? A rather lengthy answer comes to mind, but a simple one may serve your purposes better at this point. Bell System management used reinforcement weekly and at more or less random intervals during the week. Given a similar situation, you might consider doing the same.

Pros and Cons

Here, then, is a simple, demonstrably effective technique that your organization might use to its advantage. Moreover, the technique is inexpensive to employ. Supervisors will need to be trained to apply positive reinforcement correctly, and methods for collecting data will need to be developed—but such tasks are relatively inexpensive. In successful applications of positive reinforcement, these costs are repaid many times over.

In many cases, you can use positive reinforcement techniques with little or no outside help. Of course, you will want to read more about the subject than I have been able to provide here. The bibliography of suggested readings at the end of this book provides a chapter-by-chapter list of books that you might want to read, as well as their publishers' addresses.

You can turn to a consultant for help in the event that you doubt your own ability to work through a more complex situation than the one I have described, or because you lack the time to work out the details. In any case, this would not be a major undertaking.

Despite the extent to which this technique has been used successfully, it is not without its shortcomings and pitfalls. For reasons to be elaborated in the following chapter, I think it is most useful at relatively low levels of an organization and definitely of limited use at higher levels. In any event, more suitable techniques are available for improving productivity in complex jobs.

More important, once installed, the technique must be worked at continually if it is to remain effective. This really should come as no surprise, though. Your accounting system would not work if you stopped collecting or using accounting data. Thus, in positive reinforcement programs, the process of goal setting, providing feedback on goal attainment, and rewarding desired performance must be unceasing. Furthermore, as turnover and advancement bring new supervisors into your department, training must be provided to show them how they must treat their subordinates to keep the program working.

What will happen when you are transferred or promoted? Unless you train your successor and convince him or her that the program works, chances are that the program will be gradually discontinued as your people revert to traditional methods of supervision. This is why structure works best in the long run. If an innovation such as positive reinforcement is to remain an ongoing part of the organization, it must be incorporated into the organization's policies, rules, procedures, and the like. In other words, the organization's structure must be adapted to include and support the innovation.

One implication of this is that, to survive over the long run, the innovation must gain widespread use in the organization, as opposed to being used in just one of many departments. But this is easier said than done. Even though positive reinforcement is used to good effect in one department, it is not likely to be adopted voluntarily by other departments. The research indicating this to be the case is reminiscent of Frederick Taylor's story that was summarized earlier. As I indicated, time-honored but demonstrably inadequate practices often seem preferable to untried solutions to problems. At some point, management will need to encourage the innovation's use in other departments, if the innovation is to survive. But this is not the most difficult task facing management. The truly difficult part is considering alternatives to time-honored but demonstrably inadequate ways of doing things. You ought to take the time to think about this. Remember that in 20 years only one competitor took advantage of

Taylor's technique for improving productivity in the machine shop. What of the other competitors and their employees? Who ultimately was responsible for the fact that their productivity was lower than it could have been—the employees or their managers?

2

Alienated, Calculating, and Committed Workers

IS POSITIVE REINFORCEMENT
WHAT IT APPEARS TO BE?

A number of management techniques can be used to improve performance in your own organization. Although I will make my point using a few selected techniques, there literally are dozens from which to choose. Most of them work, but none of them is a panacea. How, then, can you select a technique that is likely to work with a particular group of employees?

One answer to this question can be found by investigating carefully how and why these techniques work, for the attributes of techniques that make them effective also tend to limit the variety of occasions on which they should be used. This may sound paradoxical, but a closer look at positive reinforcement provides an example that demonstrates the logic of this approach.

We can begin by being extremely skeptical of the Bell System's experience that was described in the previous chapter. As you recall, the workers were told *exactly* what management expected of them, and the subsequent performance of the workers was evaluated against management's objectives. Now, it may seem reasonable to conclude that the workers' performance improved because they were more closely supervised than they previously had been. These workers may have anticipated being punished in one way or another for performance that did not meet management's objectives, even though it was management's intention never to do this. For all we know, the possibility of being punished for substandard performance may have seemed just as real to the workers as the possibility of getting a traffic ticket for running a stop sign. Quotas, evaluations, and the unspoken threat of punishment seem to be part and parcel of traditional management practices. How, then, can anyone claim that positive reinforcement works because it is based on a theory of learning?

Actually, we ought not discount the possibility that performance will improve if we merely establish and announce goals and then measure and report each employee's performance. In fact, we will see very shortly that, under the right conditions, we should expect this sort of thing to happen because the situation described can occasionally conform to the positive reinforcement model. However, for verification that positive reinforcement is something more than traditonal management practices in disguise, we need to return to the technique's origins in a scientific laboratory, for it is in the realm of science that we will see the skeptic's argument for the straw man that it is.

How well would the "traditional management practices" argument hold up if it could be demonstrated that positive reinforcement techniques work with birds, mice, dogs, and other animals, just as well as with people? The truth of the matter is that the theory was discovered and the techniques were developed using laboratory animals, long before an attempt was made to apply the theory to the problem of changing human behavior. In one famous experiment conducted at the Yerkes Institute of Primate Psychobiology, chimpanzees were taught to work for their keep. They learned that after repeatedly lifting a heavy lever attached to a "work machine," they would receive poker chips that they could insert in a separate "vending machine" to purchase grapes and water. Some of the chimps even learned that water cost a red chip and that the price of a grape was a white chip. Blue chips, they learned, were worth two grapes.

The important thing to remember is that the chimps' behavior was learned as a result of the application of techniques similar to those used in the Bell System. That is, the behavior of interest to the experimenter was reinforced as it occurred, and the likelihood that the behavior would be repeated, thereby, was increased.

THE EFFECTIVENESS OF POSITIVE REINFORCEMENT LIMITS ITS USEFULNESS

So much for skepticism about whether the technique works as the theory says it should. Chimpanzees, birds, and mice know nothing of supervisors, management's objectives, and being written up for substandard performance. The only adequate explanation of the chimps' behavior is that behavior that is reinforced tends to be repeated.

But if this is the case, why should we expect employee performance to improve in some cases if we merely set objectives and provide feedback on the employee's subsequent performance, without rewarding the improved performance? The answer is that, in some cases, improved performance may be its own reward. If individuals are provided targets at which to aim (goals) and knowledge of how well they scored (feedback), some of them will find target practice to be intrinsically enjoyable and reinforcing. When you think about it, though, relatively few people enjoy target practice as a sport, and many employees will not be reinforced by their accomplishments at work, even after procedures for setting goals and providing feedback have been established. This observation brings us to the major issue addressed in this chapter: Which technique should you use in a particular work setting?

A prerequisite for effectively using positive reinforcement

is the ability to identify and measure the aspects of behavior to be modified. This prerequisite does not constitute a major problem when we contemplate modifying such behaviors as absenteeism, tardiness, or even the performance of simple tasks. It does constitute a problem, though, when we attempt to use the technique to alter more complex aspects of behavior —for example, when we attempt to use it to improve the quality of a manager's decisions or a scientist's research. The reason for this is apparent in the characteristics of different kinds of work. Some tasks can be performed with almost complete certainty that the objectives of the tasks will be accomplished. An assembly line epitomizes the tasks that fall into this category. We know that each job on the assembly line theoretically can be performed correctly 100 per cent of the time. In fact, this theoretical possibility has been approached in numerous firms using zero-defects programs.

These are the kinds of jobs to which positive reinforcement can be applied. We can identify all the activities that must be performed for each job of this sort, and we can measure them. The day-to-day management problem associated with supervising this kind of work is not how to accomplish it, but how to accomplish it efficiently. Cutting costs by reducing rework, simplifying procedures, and increasing output per hour of labor are the essential concerns in supervising such routine tasks.

At the other extreme are tasks that do not inevitably produce the desired results. Examples include designing and implementing an incentive system, defending a client in the courtroom, and writing a book. What such tasks have in common is that we do not know ahead of time all the activities that must be performed to achieve the intended outcomes. Because many of the behaviors that lead to successful task performance cannot be identified and measured, positive reinforcement is not an effective technique for modifying behavior and, consequently, improving task performance.

A second characteristic of work that suggests that positive reinforcement is most effective when applied to routine tasks is the length of time required to complete each unit of work.

A unit of work on an assembly line takes minutes to complete, and the assembly line worker can be rewarded for good performance many times during an eight-hour shift. Janitorial work can be completed in a single shift, and the janitors can receive reinforcement for improved performance at the end of each shift. At the other extreme, it takes months, and even years, to see the results of some management decisions; court cases often drag on for year after year; and I expect to be writing Chapter 5 sometime next summer. At what intervals should accomplishments be reinforced in these tasks—every six months or year? Reinforcement must immediately follow the behavior that is to be reinforced, but if it takes six months to find out whether an employee's performance has produced the objectives set by management, positive reinforcement probably will not work.

By now, my reasons for suggesting the use of this technique in lower level jobs should be apparent: Of all the jobs in an organization, those at the lowest levels usually are the ones in which all activities required for successful task performance can be identified and measured. Furthermore, the time required to complete a unit of work generally is short enough to permit reinforcement to be associated with specific employee behaviors.

However, I have also claimed that the technique is appropriate for alienated workers, the reason being that positive reinforcement does not require active participation on the employees' part. Each of the techniques described in subsequent chapters requires some degree of commitment, interest, and initiative from the workforce. Yet, as I have suggested, it may be rash to expect such involvement from workers who find neither pride nor pleasure in their work. Such employees are unlikely to embrace willingly the goals and aspirations of management.

Positive reinforcement can change the behavior of alienated workers because it does not depend on their conscious participation. The early successful applications of the technique were made in mental hospitals and prisons to modify the behavior of inmates and prisoners, who either lacked self-control or were deprived of control by the institutions to which they were committed. They were deviates, who rejected or failed to comprehend the laws and mores of the land. They were anything but committed, motivated organizational participants; rather, they exemplified alienation in its most extreme and tragic form.

ORGANIZATION AND ALIENATION

It is unfair, though, to portray the alienated individual as an amoral, irredeemable drone in society. First, all of us have experienced alienation in one form or another at some point in our lives. Furthermore, we frequently justify, and occasionally applaud, alienation from society. For example, the alienated and dissident inmates of the political prisons in some totalitarian regimes are viewed by democratic people as prisoners of conscience, not as criminals. Similarly, it has been suggested that alienation from the prospect of a lifetime of repetitive, boring work is understandable and even justifiable. I prefer to think of alienation as an unfortunate adaptation to an unwholesome environment. I am persuaded of this opinion by the work of a distinguished observer of modern organizations, Amitai Etzioni.[1]

Etzioni's position is that all organizations—factories, hospitals, universities, and prisons alike—face a common problem: that of controlling their members' behaviors so that organizational goals can be met. The fact that organizations are successful more often than not in controlling their members strikes most people as unremarkable. Such control is taken for granted, and the public takes notice only when the control

[1] A. Etzioni, *A Comparative Analysis of Complex Organizations*, New York: The Free Press, 1961.

is lost—when prisoners riot, students strike, or workers sabotage their factory. However, the thing that is truly remarkable is what is ignored because it is commonplace—the fact that, day in and day out, millions of people are controlled to the extent that they do essentially what their organizations demand of them. How is this degree of social control achieved with so many people so regularly, and what are its consequences for organizations and for society in general? Answers to these questions provide a way of understanding why each of the techniques to be discussed is better suited to one type of work setting than to others.

Earlier, I suggested that alienation from work is more than an immediate reaction to an unpleasant job—it is also the product of a lifetime of other experiences that predisposes an individual in this way. Other orientations toward work are shaped in this way as well. For example, there is compelling evidence in the psychological literature that a predisposition to achieve and excel at work may be a product of experiences going back to early childhood as well as a response to opportunities presented in the individual's immediate environment.

I have mentioned this merely to point out that much of the employee behavior of which we approve or disapprove was learned long before these workers were old enough to work. For such behavior, managers can take neither credit nor blame. The alienation that characterizes an employee may have its origins in the employee's childhood rather than in the practices of management, contrary to what many social critics have alleged.

Yet, some of every employee's behavior is shaped by the work environment, and this is what management has an opportunity to change for the better. Moreover, a good part of this behavior is related to the way in which employees are controlled by the organization. This is the heart of Etzioni's argument, which is summarized in the remainder of this chapter.

The Alienated Worker

One way or another, organizations control their members to the extent that the members comply with the requirements of their jobs. According to Etzioni, only three forms of control are available—coercion, remuneration, and the appeal to norms. Organizations that use coercion restrict their members' freedom with rules, procedures, and the like, and meet noncompliance with punishment. Members of such organizations cannot leave their work stations without the permission of a superior; they cannot deviate from standard procedures to vary their activities or experiment with different ways of doing their work; they cannot leave early or work late without the consent of management. They cannot break the myriad rules by which their behavior is controlled. To do so would result in being warned, written up, docked, and ultimately fired—all according to more rules.

Coercive organizations, as they are called, are typified in the extreme by prisons, correctional institutions, custodial mental hospitals, and, in less extreme cases, by parts of ordinary business organizations. The reason such organizations come to rely on the use of coercive power is that their members are alienated from the organizations' values and goals. In the extreme case, dangerous criminals are controlled by means of coercion because they cannot be relied on to exercise the degree of self-discipline required by lawful conduct. Their crimes, for which they were committed to prison, often serve as evidence of this. Appeals to society's dependency on lawful conduct or to society's norms and values have little effect on individuals whose alienation from such values has permitted them to ignore or violate them.

The less extreme case, which is of interest to us, is typified by workers who do not value their employer's objectives and who do not subscribe to the traditional belief that work has meaning and dignity. In a sense, this type of individual is described by Douglass McGregor's *Theory* X.[2] However, McGregor's position is that the behavior and attitudes in question result from the work environment that management creates for their workers. That is, if managers assume that their workers are lazy, or deceitful, or alienated, the managers will most likely develop a coercive work environment that by definition includes numerous rules, close supervision, surveillance of employee behavior, and a relatively elaborate system for disciplining individuals whose behavior does not conform to the organization's requirements. For McGregor, the worker's behavior is a direct response to a work environment that, in turn, is a manifestation of management's beliefs about the work force. Change these beliefs, McGregor argues, and management will restructure the work environment and, in so doing, elicit different kinds of behavior from the work force. Specifically, if workers are assumed to be honest, hard-working, and loyal to the company, it may occur to management that some of the organization's rules, surveillance procedures, and disciplinary processes are superfluous and, in any event, that they should be replaced by a system of management that encourages and rewards individual initiative in assuming responsibility for work. McGregor argues that if this type of change actually is made, more desirable behavior will be elicited from the work force.

McGregor's theory rests on the crucial assumption that a worker's behavior at work is determined for the most part by the work environment. However, this assumption is reasonable only in a limited sense because, as I have said, certain aspects of behavior seem to have their roots in the individual's childhood experiences. Therefore, it is implausible that a change in the nature of the job or in the way the individual is supervised will materially change the attitudes and beliefs that an individual has maintained throughout his or her life. I do not mean to suggest that these cannot change, for they can and do change over time. My argument simply is that a

[2] D. McGregor, *The Human Side of Enterprise*, New York: McGraw-Hill, 1960.

lifetime of alienation from work is not likely to be changed easily.

Etzioni's position on the control of alienated individuals is that coercion is appropriate because other means of control are inappropriate. On one hand, such individuals will not respond to appeals to social norms for the simple reason that they are alienated from these very norms. Pride in workmanship, loyalty to the organization, and the obligation to do one's best are ideas that have little meaning to an individual who does not value work. On the other hand, it is unseemly to offer to compensate such workers for doing what they are already being paid to do. For various reasons, companies cannot offer financial inducements to employees to get them to report for work on time, to avoid carelessness, or to put forth a fair day's work. To do so would amount to the moral equivalent of paying criminals to obey the law. Thus, Etzioni concludes that the remaining alternative, coercion, is the only available means by which alienated members can be controlled so that the organization can function adequately. This brings us back to McGregor's point, though, for his theory is correct in the following sense. Coercive control tends to produce alienation in those who experience it, and the situation that rendered coercion appropriate in the first place is aggravated by its use.

A fourth alternative is available—positive reinforcement— and I have recommended its use because it appears to be a more humane, more effective way of controlling the behavior of alienated workers. Moreover, its use with such individuals does not produce further alienation.

Another benefit of positive reinforcement is apparent at this point. Workers whose alienation is a culmination of experiences beginning in their youth may comprise the majority of lower-level employees in an occasional organization, but they probably constitute a relatively small fraction of the total unskilled and semiskilled work force. The majority of this segment of the work force probably is adversely affected by coercive forms of control in the sense that, although they value work, they find their current work environment to be alienating. At the least, replacing coercive control with positive reinforcement techniques may eliminate such adverse consequences.

The case for positive reinforcement is complete for the present. Positive reinforcement works best where the behaviors to be modified are relatively uncomplicated and simple to define and measure, as typified by the tasks of many unskilled and semiskilled workers. It works best when reinforcement can follow closely after the behaviors that contribute to the organization's goals. Again, tasks of brief duration typify jobs at lower levels in the organization. Positive reinforcement is a technique that can be used successfully with alienated workers, who are most likely to be found in low-level jobs. It works as well with individuals who are not alienated.

All of this boils down to two dimensions: On one hand, we are considering alienated vs. nonalienated workers and, on the other hand, we are considering simple, well-defined tasks vs. complex, ill-defined tasks. Using these two dimensions, the case for positive reinforcement can be restated as follows: Positive reinforcement is likely to be effective when the problem facing management is to improve the performance of alienated workers employed at simple, well-defined tasks. I make further use of these dimensions after we have explored alternative forms of control.

The Committed Worker

Just as some people take little pride or pleasure in their work, others are morally committed to what they do for a living. They believe in the importance of their organization, its goals, and their contributions to the organization's success. They believe in giving their best and in sticking with a job until it is finished, and they expect as much from others. Such people can be found in executive offices, but also on the shop floor in boring, repetitive jobs.

According to Etzioni, coercion is an inappropriate form of control for such workers, because there is little to be gained from attempting to coerce them into doing what they are willing to do anyway. Moreover, remuneration is not appropriate either. Offering to compensate individuals for doing what they feel morally obliged to do is a bit like offering to pay a good friend to play bridge with you. The appropriate form of control for committed employees is what Etzioni calls *normative control*—the establishment and maintenance of organizational norms and values, the use of symbols to recognize individual and group adherence to these norms, and the provision of opportunities for individuals to exemplify such values and norms.

Is normative control farfetched? I think not. A few everyday illustrations clarify what Etzioni had in mind. A number of occupational groups regularly attract individuals who can serve as models for Etzioni's committed worker. These groups include the clergy, the teaching profession, and the nursing profession, among others. People who follow such callings obviously are not avaricious. Most of them could have been better off financially had they learned a trade after graduating from high school instead of completing their baccalaureate degrees. Such occupations do not pay well because they do not need to. To be sure, nurses, teachers, and professors often complain bitterly that their salaries do not allow them to maintain adequate standards of living. Nonetheless, such complaints ought to be understood in terms of the relatively limited financial aspirations of these individuals. They are not seeking to maximize their wealth but to gain a little edge on inflation and to keep up with the office worker next door.

The qualitative difference that sets these individuals apart from the rest of the work force is the degree of their commitment to their occupations. The clergy are dedicated to their religious callings, university professors are dedicated to the pursuit and dissemination of knowledge, and nurses are dedicated to the care of the ill and infirm. Such commitment suggests that, for these individuals, remuneration is a secondary concern. Would you offer to tip a nurse in the hope that he or she might give a loved one better care? If the notion strikes you as unseemly, it is because it violates a norm that governs the profession and that is generally recognized by laypersons—

a norm requiring that a patient's needs take precedence over the nurse's self-interest.

Other occupations that attract committed workers have similar, self-regulating norms and self-imposed regulations. For example, university professors, who are dedicated to scholarship and research, will deny continued employment to an otherwise valued colleague and friend who does not contribute to the store of knowledge, a concept known as "publish or perish." Ironically, many of those who perish go on to enjoy standards of living that their former colleagues envy but will never attain.

Such dedication is regularly seen, but there are exceptions as well. We occasionally read about researchers who falsify research data in ill-fated attempts to further their self-interests. Now and then we hear about a preacher who has used church funds for personal gain. However, the fact that such occurrences are newsworthy suggests their rarity as well as the dismay with which the public regards them. More frequently, we observe lesser deviations from the norms that govern these occupations—laziness, carelessness, and faltering commitment—but such is to be expected. I once studied geography under a professor whose dedication had suffered in this regard. He was lecturing directly from his notes, telling us that the Mississippi River emptied 3.5 million gallons a minute into the Gulf of Mexico, when an athlete in the back of the room raised his hand and asked: "Gallons of what?" The professor studied his notes for several minutes and then replied: "I don't know. It doesn't say here."

Well, it doesn't say anywhere that professors will know what they are talking about or that nurses will place their patients' interests above their own, and sometimes they don't. But we take it for granted that they will because of the commitment we have learned to expect of them.

The commitment to work evidenced in these occupations can be observed in all walks of life. You probably have employees who are as dedicated to their work as teachers, in general, are to teaching. These employees are not indifferent to the amount of compensation they receive from their organization, but they can be relied on to get the job done whatever you happen to be paying them. They routinely show up for work on time because they have agreed to do so according to the terms of their employment and, more important, because they feel it would not be "right" to do otherwise. This same sense of "rightness" governs most aspects of their work. For this reason, Etzioni suggests that organizational control of committed workers is best maintained through the norms that define what is "right." The proper reward for individuals who value responsibility—who believe that they and others like them should seek responsibility in their work and their communities—is an opportunity to take on more responsibility. By the same token, employees whose commitment to their work causes them to value their accomplishments can be given further opportunities to accomplish and excel. People who accept responsibilities and opportunities without reservation become, in a sense, controlled by those responsibilities and opportunities.

Organizations that routinely employ such individuals work diligently to preserve the norms that govern the employee's behavior and to provide symbolic recognition for exemplary conduct. By way of illustration, companies that employ craftsmen are intolerant of sloppy work. Moreover, formal and informal recognition often is provided for those employees whose labors exemplify the norms of craftsmanship.

The practical suggestion to emerge from these observations is that techniques such as management by objectives, job enrichment, and various forms of participative management are most likely to be effective when used with workers who are committed to their occupations. Moreover, following Etzioni's reasoning, these techniques are more appropriately used with committed workers than are alternative techniques that are based, for example, on positive reinforcement or monetary incentives.

So far so good, but we have looked only at the alienation–commitment dimension this time. Once we add the task dimension—ill-structured–well-structured—we will be in a position to answer the question of what works when.

Earlier, I said that positive reinforcement works better when it is applied to well-structured tasks than when it is used with ill-structured tasks. Although I provided a few broad examples of tasks that fall into each category, I need to define these categories more precisely so that you will be able to judge for yourself whether a particular job falls into one category or another, or in between. For this I draw on the works of Charles Perrow.[3]

Operating an engine lathe, assembling a product, picking orders in a warehouse, and record keeping are typical well-structured jobs. For each of these jobs, we can specify all the behaviors required and the sequence in which they must be performed to complete a task successfully. In essence, we can solve all the routine problems associated with each task before the task is performed. We can do this well enough so that each of these tasks can be assigned to a computer-controlled machine. A well-structured task is one that, in theory, can be completed successfully each time it is attempted because we have planned for each element of the task and for nearly all contingencies.

Poorly structured tasks cannot be planned and completed successfully each time they are performed. Conducting scientific research, marketing a new product, selecting a manuscript for publication, and creating an advertisement typify activities that cannot be planned in such detail and with such certainty. Automobile assembly clearly fits the well-structured category, but if the 20,000 or more parts that go into a car were dumped on my office floor and if I were told to assemble them, would I be faced with a poorly structured task, or are we merely

[3] C. Perrow, *Organizational Analysis: A Sociological View.* Belmont, Calif.: Wadsworth, 1970.

talking about the complexity of different tasks? The answer to both questions is no, for we are really talking about the state of development of technology, not complexity. Look at the problem another way. If I were provided blueprints, shop manuals, and the like, given enough time, and provided an incentive that would make such a loathesome task worthwhile, I probably could assemble the parts. It might take years, but it could be done for the simple reason that the blueprints, manuals, and books would contain fairly complete descriptions of the automobile and the relationships of its various parts. Complexity can be mastered ultimately if we are working within a well-developed technology.

Poorly structured tasks are not well understood, and we do not have an adequate technology for performing them. Thus, they cannot be planned by one individual and performed according to plan by another. Rather, planning for the task proceeds as the task is being performed, and such planning is altered according to the way the task progresses. An attorney cannot prepare a script for the entire defense of a client because what the lawyer does in court depends in part on what happens in court. By the same token, we can find jobs at all levels of an organization that cannot be planned for in detail. The successful performance of these jobs depends on the job holders' ability to make judgments about contingencies that arise as the jobs progress. Bear in mind that *judgment* is the important word here. Mere contingencies often can be planned for. In the case of poorly structured problems, however, we lack the technology to develop logical solutions for each contingency, and we must rely on judgment or some equivalent such as experience, intuition, or artistry. It is disconcerting to think that complex organizations rely on anything other than facts and logic, but they must do so as often as not. Counseling a problem employee, devising a marketing plan, and writing copy for an advertising campaign hinge on crucial problems for which logical solutions do not exist.

With these definitions in mind, we are in a position to arrive at the logic that will help in deciding when it is appropriate to use a certain technique. In Figure 2–1, the two dimensions that have been discussed are combined to form a

Figure 2–1
Work Settings and Appropriate Techniques

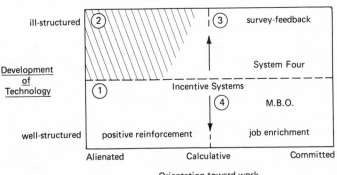

two-by-two table. The horizontal dimension, *alienation–commitment*, describes an individual's orientation toward work. The vertical dimension, *ill-structured–well-structured*, describes the state of development of the technology used to accomplish the task in question. Obviously, the two dimensions are present in all human labors, and for convenience we will say that the two define a work setting.

The work setting described by Quadrant 1 of the table is the familiar case of the alienated worker performing a well-structured task that has been discussed in some detail and needs no further elaboration. Quadrant 2 defines a theoretically possible, but improbable, work setting. It is quite unlikely that an organization will delegate responsibility for solving ill-structured problems to employees who are alienated from work. It is equally improbable that such workers will aspire to such responsibilities, and we need not consider the matter further.

Quadrant 4 describes work settings in which relatively committed workers perform well-structured tasks. To the extent that such individuals aspire to responsibility, a sense of accomplishment, and the like, techniques such as job enrichment will be effective. Job enrichment, which is discussed in detail later on, entails combining fragmented tasks to form a larger, more demanding and rewarding job. When job enrichment is performed correctly, tasks are combined in such a way that the worker has a role in planning the work to be accomplished as well as responsibility for the results of the work.

By combining separate tasks into an entire job, the worker is given greater responsibility and a greater sense of accomplishment.

Job enrichment seems to work best where a number of discrete tasks can be combined into a single, larger job. However, if we consider jobs that require the use of increasingly ill-structured technologies, we see that the possibility of successfully identifying and combining tasks becomes progressively remote, and job enrichment becomes less and less attractive. At some point, we will be better off if we focus our attention on objectives rather than means. Thus, techniques such as management by objectives (MBO) are advocated for work settings in which the technology is not well-structured and, consequently, does not permit us to aggregate specific tasks into larger jobs. Unlike well-structured jobs in which the contribution of each task to the end product can be established with a degree of certainty, the means–ends relationships in ill-structured tasks are not nearly as clear-cut. Thus, rather than provide more tasks for the individual, it is better to provide more goals and permit the individual to select and adapt his or her means to achieve those goals as circumstances suggest. Essentially, this is what MBO is about. Managers and subordinates discuss and agree on the subordinates' goals for a period to come, and the managers assume responsibility for helping their subordinates achieve these goals. In this way, subordinates who want more responsibility can take it on by setting new goals for themselves. Furthermore, they are permitted discretion in determining how these objectives will be met.

By now, you may be thinking of people you know who have all the responsibility they want or need. What they need is not more goals or bigger jobs but help in finding ways to discharge more effectively the responsibilities they already have. As a rule, the jobs of such people are extremely ill structured. The following illustration shows that both MBO and job enrichment are inappropriate in such cases.

Imagine a supervisor who is faced with the following problems: Production in her unit is off 12 per cent for the month, and management wants an explanation as well as a remedy. One of her best workers has sought her counsel in a personal matter that involves major emotional consequences. Notice has just come through that the current production run will be stopped in order for her department to begin work on a high-priority order. Two of her subordinates are absent today, and their temporary replacements have not shown up. And she has a union grievance hearing to attend in 35 minutes. Her situation has three attributes of extremely ill-structured jobs: (1) the majority of problems that confront the job holder lack logical, predefined solutions; (2) moreover, many of these problems are interrelated in that a solution to one problem may affect, and even aggravate, other problems; and (3) problems arise unpredictably. When objectives change unpredictably, techniques such as MBO have limited usefulness. Furthermore, when people do not know how to deal adequately with the responsibilities they have, adding even more responsibilities, such as through a program of job enrichment, may be detrimental to both their productivity and morale.

This supervisor's situation illustrates the work setting described in Quadrant 3 of Figure 2–1. The techniques for improving productivity in this quadrant basically involve problem solving through participation. Participative problem solving is reasonable to consider whenever committed employees are involved as participants. Furthermore, group problem solving is appropriate for ill-structured problems for two reasons. First, ill-structured problems often stem from organizational or group functioning. In the foregoing illustration, one part of the organization is demanding efficiency in production while another part is demanding the flexibility to alter production runs. The tradeoffs involved in meeting either demand are likely to be ignored unless explicitly raised as a problem with the appropriate group of managers and supervisors. Second, when judgment is needed, the adage that two (or more) heads are better than one applies. Group problem solving is advocated for ill-structured problems, particularly when they arise from functions of the group.

The development and application of participative management techniques have resulted in an interesting and promising source of solutions to age-old management problems. I cannot dwell on them here, but will discuss these techniques at length in Chapter 6. For the present, we need to return to Figure 2–1 to investigate its center, where the four work settings overlap one another. In doing this, we return to Etzioni's work and complete his argument.

The Calculative Worker

We generally agree to what is meant by a commitment to work-related values, and alienation is understood to describe an active rejection of such values. What happens, though, when an individual neither embraces nor rejects these values but merely is indifferent to them? This condition is termed *anomie*—from the Greek word, *anomos*, which means without law. In our sense it means without norms or values—without a belief in the "rightness" or "wrongness" of actions or thoughts.

What can be said of people who, without threat of coercion, willingly pursue activities that, to them, are without value? We can only say that they are using means to pursue other ends. In organizations, anomie manifests itself in the attitude that a job is a means of achieving personal gratification—power, money, or status—and little more. Employees who are predisposed to this way of thinking often perform well as long as good performance results in adequate remuneration. However, they usually lack loyalty to the organization and dedication to its goals, and such workers are more than willing to quit a present job to work for a higher bidder.

Evidence of anomie is plentiful in organizations of every sort. "Empire builders" strive for power, status, and higher salaries even though their empire building is detrimental to the organization's performance. Foot draggers slow down the job, not because they dislike their work, but because they want the overtime that results. "What's in it for me?" comes out before, "When do you need it?" On the positive side of such employees, bonuses spur levels of productivity that cannot be attained under straight salary systems, and employee suggestion systems bring forth good ideas that, in the absence of compensation, usually go unspoken.

There is nothing intrinsically wrong with viewing a job as a means to financial ends. Although we probably prefer commitment over anomie in the work force, it must be recalled that in a free enterprise system labor operates in a market for labor where wages are a function of supply and demand. Thus, the employee who is primarily concerned about the *quids* and *quos* of his job is not much different from the firm's owner, who is viewed as being rightfully concerned about costs and revenues.

The point is merely that anomie results in employee behavior that constitutes a different set of problems for management from those posed by either alienation or commitment. According to Etzioni, neither coercion nor normative control is appropriate in such cases. Norms and values are without meaning where anomie prevails. Moreover, coercive control is unnecessary because more effective inducements are available. A preferred mechanism for controlling workers such as these is a compensation system that explicitly matches inducements to employee productivity.

Numerous incentive systems have been used successfully over the years. Simple piece-rate systems have been used for well-structured jobs, and more elaborate systems have been developed to provide incentives for workers in ill-structured jobs. However, for every successful application of an incentive system, there are numerous examples of unsuccessful attempts. Why these systems work and why they sometimes fail is the topic of the next chapter.

3

Calculating
Workers

AN INCENTIVE TO PRODUCE

What works needs to be worked at. Organizations that work to improve their techniques for increasing productivity find those techniques to be effective. The following review of the history of a simple incentive program that was started in 1953 and that is still in use illustrates this point.[1]

The year is 1951, and the organization is the Water Meter Division of the Philadelphia Water Department. The building that houses the Water Meter Division is dirty and cheerless, and the prospects facing the division are even more melancholy.

The division is responsible for maintaining the city's 320,000 water meters by repairing malfunctioning units and overhauling all meters periodically according to a preventive maintenance schedule. Some malfunctioning meters are repaired in the field, but those requiring extensive repairs, as well as the meters due for periodic overhaul, are returned to the shop.

[1] J. M. Greiner, R. E. Dahl, H. P. Hatry, and A. P. Millar. *Monetary Incentives and Work Standards in Five Cities*. Washington, D.C.: The Urban Institute, 1977.

Most work in the shop is similar to assembly line work, except that the employees control the pace of work. There is no conveyor to move work from one work station to the next. Rather, meters are passed from one employee to the next as each stage in the repair process is accomplished. Disassembled meters go into the inventory of the worker who cleans them; cleaned meters join the inventory awaiting inspection; and so on through repair, testing, and painting.

Although most of the department's customers have metered service, some Philadelphians pay a flat monthly rate for their water, which is based on the number of faucets, toilets, and the like in the customer's building. At the time our story begins, the city has decided to provide metered service for all customers. Flat-rate billing will be phased out as an additional 180,000 meters are installed. Installation of these meters will constitute a major problem for the Water Meter Division, which presently has a backlog of 35,000 meters in need of repair or overhaul. The division has considered investing $350,000 to relocate and expand the repair shop.

Rather than invest in a larger facility, though, management has decided to increase the productivity of the existing shop by introducing an incentive payment system that is simple and straightforward. Work-measurement techniques are to be used to establish time standards for each operation in the repair process. For example, if it is determined that an average employee working at a normal pace can clean 48 meters in an eight-hour day, then the standard time for this operation will be defined as 10 minutes per meter. Workers who produce at the standard rate or below (48 or fewer operations per shift, in our example) are to be guaranteed their base wage. Workers who produce at a rate in excess of the standard are to be paid a bonus that is calculated as follows. Suppose that the worker in our example earns $5.00 per hour and produces 60 units in an eight-hour shift. When we multiply the units produced by the standard time required to produce each unit we find:

$$60 \text{ units} \times 10 \text{ minutes/unit} = 600 \text{ minutes} = 10 \text{ hours}$$

The worker's output would have been produced in 10 hours had he worked at the standard rate. In effect, our worker has "earned" two additional hours during his eight-hour shift. Thus, he will be paid for the 10 hours worth of work he produced rather than for the eight hours he actually worked, and his earnings will amount to $50.00—a 25 per cent bonus over what he would have earned at the standard base wage.

Now, suppose the worker in our example produced only 48 units having the same standard time of 10 minutes per unit. His earnings calculated under the incentive plan will be the same as his earnings when calculated according to his base wage. If we multiply the 48 units produced by the 10 minutes required to complete each unit we will find that his output would have been produced in 480 minutes had he worked at the standard rate:

$$48 \text{ units} \times 10 \text{ minutes/units} = 480 \text{ minutes} = 8 \text{ hours}$$

Now, 480 minutes is eight hours. Thus, the worker's earnings are calculated by multiplying his base wage of $5.00 per hour by the eight hours. His earnings, then, are $40.00. Remember that he can earn at least this much regardless of how few units he produces. The general formulas for computing incentive earnings, standard earnings, and the incentive bonus as a percentage of standard earnings are as follows:

Incentive Earnings

Units produced × standard hours/unit = earned hours
Earned hours × base wage/hour = incentive earnings

Standard Earnings

Hours worked × base wage/hour = standard earnings

Incentive Bonus as a Percentage of Standard Earnings

$$\frac{\text{Incentive earnings} - \text{standard earnings}}{\text{Standard earnings}} = \text{Percentage of Bonus}$$

In all cases, an inspector will check the operation and accuracy of the meters before they leave the shop. Faulty meters will be returned for rework to the employees whose work is defective, and it will not be included in the employee's output for the shift.

TAILORING THE TECHNIQUE
TO THE ORGANIZATION

When management must tailor the incentive program to fit the organization, the program will lose some of its elegance. First, in the case of meter repairs, there is the problem of field personnel who make repairs on the customers' premises. Although management will implement an incentive plan for these individuals, the plan will be modified to include a provision for unproductive calls to premises that cannot be entered because the occupants are absent. Next, not all the meters repaired in the shop are of the same design. Some are complicated and are repaired by more qualified repair personnel who work independently rather than as part of a repair team. Such work is quite varied and, consequently, does not lend itself readily to the techniques of work measurement. Thus, these jobs will be excluded from the incentive plan. However, the wages of these skilled workers and those of the inspectors will be increased to compensate for the perceived inequity that may result as less skilled repair personnel begin to earn incentive bonuses. Finally, some semiskilled jobs, such as painting the repaired meters, will be excluded from the incentive plan, but these workers will be permitted to take turns working at jobs covered by the plan in order to earn occasional incentive bonuses.

Finally, there is the union to contend with. Before the plan is implemented, management will concede three points: that employees will not be laid off if increased productivity resulting from the plan renders some of them redundant; that employees who produce below standard will be guaranteed their base wages; and that standards, as determined by work measurement techniques, will be "cushioned" by 25 per cent to permit most employees to earn incentive bonuses. In addition, the city's Civil Service Commission will insist that the entire program be reviewed at four- to five-year intervals, at which times standards will be redetermined. An examination and discussion of the plan follows shortly, but for now it seems that the first two concessions were reasonable but that the third may have been potentially disastrous. The Civil Service Commission's insistence on periodic reviews of the program may have remedied over time the concession on standards. Standards should be determined by empirical data. If you can establish by valid measurements that it takes 10 minutes to complete a task, why should you agree in a negotiation session that it takes 12½ minutes? The argument that such measures are imprecise does not, by itself, constitute a rationale for relaxing standards because errors in measurement can occur in both directions. Yet it is not uncommon for such concessions to be made by management in return for union acceptance of a plan.

THE RESULTS

When the incentive program was installed, it was explained to the employees so that they would be able to calculate their own incentive bonuses if they chose to do so. Moreover, incentive bonuses were posted in the shop each payday. On the average, workers were able to earn 17 per cent bonuses.

By 1975 some rather impressive results had accrued to the program. Although the number of meters in service per repair employee had increased 162 per cent since 1952, the backlog of work had declined from 35,000 meters to none. The number of repair employees covered by the plan decreased during the period from 47 to 28, and the workload of each employee had increased 23 per cent. The department estimates that it has saved $142,000 per year net of program costs (in 1967 dollars) between 1967 and 1975 as a result of such increased efficiencies. Other benefits are apparent as well.

Periodic reviews of the program have led to innovations and improvements in work methods and work flows. As a result, the time needed to repair a meter has been reduced to 31 minutes from 86 minutes in 1953.

Yet, not all of these improvements can be attributed solely to the incentive program. Numerous other changes occurred between 1953 and 1975, and these changes undoubtedly contributed to the department's efficiency. For example, field crews were reduced from two employees to one; magnetic meters, having fewer parts and requiring less time to repair than the older, mechanical ones, began to replace existing equipment; and the period between scheduled routine maintenance of meters was extended from 10 to 15 years. Each change materially affected productivity, but all occurred within the context of the incentive program. We cannot isolate the effects of these changes from the effects of the program itself. We can agree, though, that a well-managed incentive program can increase and sustain productivity for many years.

HOW AN INCENTIVE PROGRAM WORKS

A variety of incentive programs has been developed over the years. Some are as simple as the one employed by the Water Meter Division, whereas others are quite complex, involving hundreds of employees and dozens of job categories. Nonetheless, all such programs can be explained by a simple theory of motivation. Moreover, the theory not only illustrates how these programs work; it also explains why they sometimes fail to perform as expected. Essentially, the theory tells us how people think about the alternatives facing them.

Thinking is hard work. A great deal of what we do, consequently, is done without a great deal of thought—absent-mindedly, as it were. This is not to say that we are thoughtless people. When confronted with alternatives that have material outcomes, we sometimes think through each alternative before selecting a single course of action. As an illustration, take the case of an employee on a loading dock who gives little or no thought to the question of how productive he should be. To be sure, he discovered when he first started working that he could neither work too slowly nor too quickly. Working too slowly got him in trouble with the foreman; working too quickly created problems with his co-workers. Besides, working quickly was tiring. However, between "too slowly" and "too quickly" there exists a fairly broad range of performance levels that our dock worker does not explicitly consider. He may work at a comfortable pace for a while, then stop to have a cigarette, and then work rather leisurely while he talks with a co-worker. You might say that his pace of work is controlled by the other things he wants to do while he works. Moreover, he does not bother to think about alternative, more efficient, ways in which he could do his job. Within relatively broad limits, there are no consequences to him for working quickly or slowly and efficiently or inefficiently. Because such alternatives are without consequences, why should he seriously consider them?

Now let us alter the illustration by introducing a simple incentive payment program similar to the one used in the Water Meter Division. An outline of the program is depicted in Figure 3–1. In this example, we have developed a standard time for a unit of work (unloading a shipment), and we have guaranteed the worker his base wage rate for substandard performance. Incentive earnings for performance that exceeds the standard will be calculated as they were in the Water Meter Division.

By introducing the incentive earnings program, we have created a situation in which alternative levels of productivity will have material consequences for our hypothetical employee —consequences he will want to consider. How such alternatives are considered is explained by a theory of motivation developed by Victor Vroom. In simplified form, the theory suggests that our worker will explore four major aspects of the situation with which he has been confronted.[2]

First, he will think through the relationship between his level of performance and the outcome of immediate concern—

[2] Victor Vroom, *Work and Motivation.* New York: Wiley, 1964.

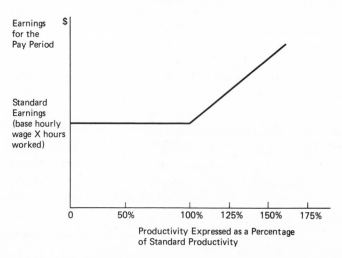

Figure 3–1

A Simple Incentive Payment Program

increased productivity. There is much to examine here. On the one hand, there are estimates that suggest that average employees paid hourly produce only 50 to 60 per cent of what they are capable of producing. On the other hand, there are situations in which working harder will not necessarily accomplish more. If the theory is correct, our worker will spend some time investigating the extent to which effort is related to productivity in his job. For example, he will ask himself whether a modest improvement in performance will require an inordinate amount of effort. In addition, there is a limit to every worker's ability to produce, and a thoughtful employee will attempt to determine this limit in order to evaluate the maximum potential benefits to be gained from the incentive program.

Second, the employee will examine the value of different levels of performance in terms of their numerous immediate outcomes. At some point, working harder may lead to some unpleasant consequences such as fatigue, boredom, the inability to socialize with co-workers, and the like. The trade-offs involved are important to some workers and affect their ultimate behavior.

Third, our worker will contemplate the value he places on the ultimate outcome associated with increased productivity—the incentive bonus. Although a dollar is a dollar, each of us places a slightly different subjective value on the opportunity to earn an additional dollar. Some employees will be extremely motivated by the chance to increase their take-home pay whereas others, for reasons we do not fully understand, will be indifferent.

Finally, there is the important question of the relationship between the immediate outcome—increased productivity—and the ultimate outcome—increased earnings. This is not a simple matter because at one level of productivity the relationship between productivity and earnings may be positive over the long run whereas at a higher level of productivity this relationship may be zero, or even negative. We will see the logic of this by examining the incentive program through our dockworker's eyes.

Suppose that the employee produces at 120 per cent of standard. He will earn a 20 per cent incentive bonus, management will realize a 20 per cent increase in his productivity without having made additional investments in plant or equipment, and all concerned should be satisfied.

Now the question arises: Will our worker be as optimistic about the potential consequences of producing 160 per cent of standard? For one thing, a 60 per cent increase in earnings may destroy the differential between the worker's pay and his supervisor's and, in so doing, interfere with the notion that salaries should vary according to the individual's position in the organization's hierarchy of authority. What is worse, the 60 per cent increase in productivity may be interpreted by management as an indication that the standard for the job was set at an unrealistically low level. Our worker will contemplate these ideas along with the likelihood that management will respond by restudying the job and, as a result, increasing the standard. This isn't quite cricket. Management probably will not restudy the job. Rather, the job will probably be redesigned, and *then* it will be restudied. The result is the same in any event. Our worker will conclude that he may wind up working harder under the tighter standard than he previously had to work under the old standard to earn the same incentive bonus. This is an illustration of a situation in which the relationship between productivity and earnings can become negative in the long run. An anticipated outcome of a high level of productivity is an alteration of the incentive program that will result in a smaller incentive bonus for the same high level of productivity.

All things considered, our hypothetical employee is likely to conclude that the best thing for his co-workers and him to do will be to peg production somewhere between 15 and 20 per cent above standard. By doing this, they will earn fairly substantial bonuses while avoiding the fatigue that can accompany higher levels of performance. Moreover, they will keep from management the knowledge that productivity could be even greater, and management will not suspect that standards are slack.

It is important to note that production is also pegged by workers who are paid by the hour, but this occurs for reasons other than the ones described here. Yet in all cases, whether pegging or restricting exists, management should not automatically interpret either as a symptom of some moral flaw or of alienation from work. Rather, given what such employees believe to be true of management, their behavior may result from their intelligent, calculative assessments of the situation at hand—the alternatives available to them and the likely outcomes of such alternatives. In other words, such behavior evidences thought processes similar to those used by management in assessing the alternatives available to the organization.

One more point is in order. The strategy our hypothetical worker has chosen will be successful only if all workers covered by the incentive plan agree to use it. If several employees decide, instead, to produce as much as they can and maximize their earnings, the attempt to keep management ignorant of the workers' ability to produce will not succeed. Thus, it is not uncommon for workers to establish group norms that strictly define what will be considered as acceptable behavior. Furthermore, such norms permit sanctions of various kinds to be employed when a group member violates the norms. In our example, a norm may develop that defines producing above a certain percentage of standard as unacceptable behavior. Consistently producing below the standard may be defined as unacceptable behavior as well. Bear in mind that these norms protect a rational strategy for maximizing the welfare of the work group. Individuals who disregard such norms jeopardize the welfare of the group. Newcomers are particularly likely to disregard norms because they are naive and do not understand the rationales for such strategies or because they choose to place their own welfare above that of the group. The sanctions used to enforce the norms of a work group begin with attempts to educate the new employee. However, the sanctions can escalate in severity when the newcomer is slow or unwilling to learn, and the recalcitrant worker may be ostracized by the group, threatened, and, in rare instances, physically abused. Ultimately, the sanctions work, and the newcomer usually conforms or finds another job.

INCENTIVES AND DISINCENTIVES

Once again, we have seen that the very factors that explain a technique's usefulness also tend to limit its effectiveness. A technique that theoretically could increase productivity by as much as 100 per cent may produce only a 15 to 20 per cent increase in practice—all because of the workers' thoroughness in thinking through the implications of producing at different levels.

Even a 15 per cent increase in productivity (and incentive earnings) may represent a substantial improvement for the organization and its employees, and it may be that your organization could improve performance in some jobs through the use of incentive payment systems that achieve no more than a 15 per cent increase in productivity. However, by carefully managing an incentive plan you may be able to achieve even better results. Of course, the opposite is true, as well, and a poorly managed plan most likely will result in failure. I will elaborate in the next few pages the major management problems associated with the type of incentive plan that has been discussed. Before doing that, though, I want to digress for a moment to raise a related, important issue—disincentives.

Some years ago, I was standing at a crosswalk in New Orleans, waiting for a traffic light to change. Next to me stood a blind man and his Seeing Eye dog. As I waited, I watched the dog, who, to my dismay, abruptly snarled and bit his master on the leg. In disbelief, I watched as the blind man took a candy bar from his coat pocket, unwrapped it, and held it out to his dog. Unable to contain myself, I said to the man, "You aren't going to reward the dog with food after he bit you, are you?" "No," he said. "I'm just trying to find out where his mouth is, so I can kick him in the other end."

This was an example of a management technique that has survived intact across the ages—a good kick in the pants when things aren't going according to plan. The use of this technique has become much more subtle over the years, the unions having had good effect in this regard. Most labor contracts protect the employee by restraining management's urge to kick, as it were.

It is important to note that neither of the techniques presented so far relies on disincentives nor do any of the techniques to be discussed subsequently. There are occasions when it is appropriate to use disincentives, but these are drastic occasions. Punishment in any form is not a particularly useful or desirable means for increasing productivity, and the reasons are quite clear when the employees' reactions to disincentives are examined using Vroom's Theory. This is illustrated by altering slightly the preceding examples of incentive programs. In these examples, it was made clear to employees that they would not be penalized if their productivity fell below the standard level. This policy recognizes that workers do not have absolute control over their productivity. Occasionally, their machines break down, work-in-process inventories become depleted, and raw materials are defective. In none of these cases would management want to penalize the workers. Yet it would be naive to assume that all substandard performance results from conditions over which the worker has no control;

there also are occasions when substandard performance results from willful acts. Such actions can make life difficult for the first-line supervisor, who may suspect that a substantial amount of the substandard productivity in his department actually results from malingering or soldiering. For this reason, the supervisor in our example has made it a practice to berate and admonish workers when they do not produce up to standard. Although they are not penalized financially for poor performance, the workers are subjected to considerable unpleasantness.

The workers know that their performance will not remain uniformly above standard. There will be occasional days when they run out of parts, and there will be other occasions when they just do not feel like working. Thus, they will devise a strategy for avoiding their supervisor's displeasure when they produce below standard. Once again, the relationships between different levels of performance and the immediate outcomes associated with these will be evaluated, as will the value these outcomes have for the workers. For example, a worker who is feeling out of sorts may conclude that he values avoiding fatigue more than he values a high level of productivity that would result in fatigue. And there are tradeoffs to consider between immediate and ultimate outcomes. Substandard performance will lead to a day's pay at the hourly rate but also to the loss of potential incentive earnings and possibly to an unpleasant scene with the supervisor.

The fourth step in Vroom's Theory provides the worker with a way out of this dilemma. In evaluating the relationship between immediate outcomes (e.g., productivity) and ultimate outcomes (e.g., incentive earnings or reprimands), the worker will realize that such links are neither inevitable nor immutable. The worker's way out of the dilemma is to reduce to an acceptable level the probability that he will be made to suffer adverse consequences for substandard performance.

On a good day our worker may feel like turning out 150 per cent of standard. He won't do this, of course—or will he? Suppose that he produces 50 per cent above standard one day but turns in only 80 per cent of his output. By doing this, he

now has a bank of completed work from which to draw on
the days when his productivity falls below standard. The bank
enables him to maintain his accustomed 20 per cent incentive
bonus on a day when he produces only 90 per cent of standard.
Alternatively, he can turn in standard production on a day
when his output has fallen to 70 per cent of standard. In both
cases, the link between substandard production and a repri-
mand from the supervisor would be broken.

Our dock worker is clever, though, and when he first
conceives of this strategy, he realizes that the crucial problem
is to find a way to hide his bank. Banking small parts in a
machine shop is one thing, but hiding empty box cars is quite
another. As he thinks about the problem, the solution becomes
obvious. He and his co-workers become a "bank" in the sense
that they coordinate and keep track of transfers of productivity. For example, when he produces more than 120 per cent
of standard, our worker contributes some of his "earned" hours
to the group. These hours are made available to other group
members who do not meet the standard that day. Then, on a
day when our worker is out of sorts and produces little, he is
able to reclaim the hours he has contributed previously. In
this way the problem of hiding the "bank" is solved.

The point is simple enough. Disincentives often produce
ways that enable employees to avoid the disincentives rather
than producing the kinds of behavior management wished to
produce. When you think about the employees' thoughtfulness
and ingenuity that go into these avoidance strategies, it is
apparent that organizations that systematically employ disincentives would be far better off searching for ways in which such
ingenuity could be turned to the organization's advantage.

MANAGING THE INCENTIVE PROGRAM

The care and thoughtfulness that management exercises in the
development of an incentive program are repaid many times
over. The ultimate success or failure of such programs usually
can be traced back to the adequacy of the initial designs.

Ironically, the most costly mistakes that can occur in such designs are usually the obvious ones.

Take, for example, the problem of deciding on a measure of employee productivity. Obviously, it is essential to use incentive rewards only for output over which the employee has direct control. Yet, I have seen incentive plans that were designed to reward output over which the employees had little or no control. The failure of such plans is predictable.

A related problem arises when individual incentive plans are installed where group plans are more appropriate. In such cases, attempts to maximize individual productivity may be detrimental to the group's overall productivity. Just as athletes place teamwork above individual achievement, workers who function as a team must subjugate the performance of individuals to the group's efforts. Incentive plans that reward group productivity encourage a team effort whereas those based on the output of individuals usually do not.

Difficulties are sometimes encountered in defining and measuring output. Many kinds of work defy attempts to construct adequate measures of productivity; they do not lend themselves to the kind of incentive program described here. Obviously, it is unreasonable to attempt to use so-called piecework incentive systems to measure the productivity of employees who work at extremely complex tasks, or whose tasks vary greatly, or whose tasks that entail the application of ill-structured technologies. However, even seemingly simple clerical jobs such as word processing often defy incorporation into incentive programs. For example, it is extremely difficult to develop and implement standards for a typist, who may produce letters, tables, reports, and manuscripts that contain prose, mathematical equations, and data matrices. Some of these difficulties can be overcome by group incentive programs that reward productivity as measured according to criteria that are more global than individual task performance. Systems that promote teamwork are the topic of Chapter 4.

Computation of incentive bonuses can become intricate and time-consuming if such difficulties are not anticipated by management. Recall that incentive programs frequently are referred to as piecework plans, although the term is often misused. Piecework implies a specific form of incentive program—one that was popularized in Frederic Taylor's time. Piecework refers to the practice of paying workers a specified amount of money for each unit of work performed. There is nothing intrinsically wrong with such arrangements. However, each time the basic wage structure changes—for example, when the minimum wage is increased or when labor contracts are renegotiated—piecework rates must be adjusted accordingly. If hundreds, or even dozens, of units of work are covered by a plan, the effort required to redetermine rates will be time-consuming and costly. This is why incentive programs typically use the standard time approach that has been described earlier; this approach accommodates changes in the wage structure by holding time standards consistent. All that is needed when wage rates change is a substitution of the new rate for the old one in the formulas used to calculate incentive earnings.

However, work standards must change over the long run, regardless of the type of incentive plan used. As new tools and work methods are introduced, workers will become more efficient, and prevailing standards will be rendered inaccurate. What is less apparent is that standards tend to "go soft" over time, even when methods and machinery are unchanged. This happens for many reasons, and not all of them can be described here. However, a brief look at a few of the typical reasons is enlightening.

Many changes occur unnoticed in organizations. Suppliers of raw materials improve their products over time. Subassemblies that go into a fabrication process are improved by the subsidiary organization that builds them. Workers become more skilled and, thus, more efficient at their jobs. These and related changes combine to reduce the time required to perform the various tasks covered by the incentive program. Because the changes occur gradually and because they sometimes originate in other organizations or departments—as is the case with improved subassemblies—they often are not apparent to management. Thus, work standards go soft, and standard times that once were challenging to exceed eventually become child's play to master.

Standards should be regularly reviewed and, when appropriate, revised at regular intervals. As you might expect, though, employees are likely to resist, or at least resent, such changes. There is no doubt that when standards are tightened, employees must work harder for a given amount of incentive bonus than they did under the old standards. This is quite similar to the situation described earlier in which attempts to peg productivity were explained. In this case, though, management's intentions appear to be justified by fairness, and this perception of fair play can be used to eliminate or at least reduce the employees' resentment of management's efforts to redefine standards.

The groundwork for dealing with employee resistance to change should be incorporated in the original design of the incentive program, as is apparent from studies of employee satisfaction and dissatisfaction.[3] Basically, feelings of resentment or acceptance and dissatisfaction or satisfaction are related to an employee's initial expectations about the situation. For example, if you expect to be promoted two years from now, you probably will not be dissatisfied if you are not promoted next year. On the other hand, if you expect to be promoted next year, but two years pass before promotion comes, you may feel that you have been badly treated by the organization. The objective event—promotion in two years—may be the same in either case. What is different is the subjective event—that is, your expectation concerning promotion.

It can be shown that resistance to changes in standards may be successfully anticipated if the employees understand that work standards almost invariably go soft and that for this reason they must be reviewed at regular intervals. Such understanding should be nurtured prior to the implementation of an incentive plan and systematically reinforced thereafter, for it is easy enough to forget what is potentially unpleasant. This won't stop the griping and gnashing of teeth that will echo throughout the plant when the time to review standards

[3] R. A. Ullrich, A *Theoretical Model of Human Behavior in Organizations*. Morristown, N.J.: General Learning Press, 1972.

arrives, but it may eliminate the widespread feeling of unfair-
ness that can accompany changes that are unexpected and
without apparent rationale.

Another, related problem remains to be solved. It is an
old problem with tragic consequences that comes into sharpest
relief in connection with another type of employee compensation. *Tally's Corner*, an early study of the effects of ghetto life,
recounted a vicious cycle of assumptions and events that
inevitably produced a sordid, self-fulfilling prophecy.[4] Ghetto
employers, it seemed, learned from experience that their employees could be counted on to steal from them. Knowing
approximately how much would be stolen each week by the
average employee, the employers adjusted the wage structure
downward to allow for the predictable amount of theft. According to Elliot Liebow, the author of *Tally's Corner*, the
resulting wage structures were approximately equal to those
outside of the ghetto less anticipated losses due to employee
theft.

However, according to Liebow, the resulting ghetto wage
was not a living wage. It did not allow the average worker to
provide adequately for a family, even according to the dismal
standards of adequacy that prevailed in the Washington, D.C.
ghetto. Consequently, these workers either stole enough from
their employers to get by or asked their employers why they
were paid less than people who held similar jobs outside the
ghetto. Those who asked were likely to be told that they were
paid less because they stole from their bosses. If someone is
paid less than the going rate because that person is expected
to steal the difference, then there is a perverse sort of justifica-
tion for stealing. The irony of this situation shades off into
tragedy because otherwise decent people are subtly coerced
into petty crime.

A parallel to this situation arises in connection with
establishing and evaluating work standards. Self-interest may
lead some workers to slow down as their productivity is being
measured to establish standards. The time-study people who

---

[4] E. Liebow, *Tally's Corner*. Boston: Little, Brown, & Co., 1967.

are experienced in developing such standards realize this, and they sometimes allow for slowdowns by systematically reducing their measures of standard times. But workers also learn from experience. Even scrupulously honest workers may slow down somewhat when their jobs are being studied because they have learned to expect that the people who study jobs routinely shave points off their empirical data. Shades of *Tally's Corner!* As does the common cold, this organization ill awaits a cure.

The final problem to be discussed in connection with simple incentive plans is determining the size of the incentive bonus to be paid. Clearly, there are alternatives to paying an extra hour's wage for each standard hour "earned," and each alternative has its own consequences.

A number of so-called "sharing plans" divide incentive gains between the workers and management. Some plans provide a 50–50 split, whereas others are somewhat less generous to the workers. On the other hand, there are plans that provide increasing incentive bonuses for increasing levels of productivity. One such plan, depicted in Figure 3–2, has been used for many years by a large sales organization. According to the plan, sales representatives are paid a modest salary for serving their existing accounts. In addition, they

Figure 3–2

A Sales Incentive Plan With Increasing Incentive Bonuses

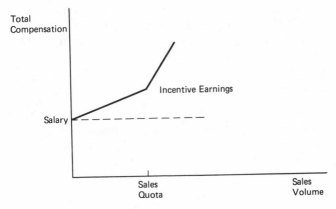

receive a monthly commission on the dollar volume of the sales they produce. However, the commission they can earn increases dramatically as a percentage of sales, after a given volume of sales has been achieved for the year. The intent and effect of this plan are to encourage exceptionally high levels of performance. Similar plans have been used with manufacturing personnel. The major attribute of these plans is that they signal clearly to employees that pegging production is uncalled for, that management will pay handsomely for exceptionally high levels of productivity.

Which type of plan should you use? It depends on the conditions your organization faces. If a sharing plan provides adequate financial inducements to maintain productivity at the level the organization needs, then it probably is better to use that type of plan than one of the alternatives. However, the problem of deciding on an adequate level of incentive compensation is by no means a simple one.

What level of productivity does the organization need? Can it use everything it produces? If it can, the organization may profit from implementing a plan that attempts to maximize productivity. However, organizations sometimes are unable to use everything they produce. It may not pay a company to produce more than it can sell or to produce more subassemblies than finished products. Thus, an organization may prefer a plan that yields a modest increase in productivity to an alternative that attempts to maximize output.

What are the alternatives to a given plan? Should a company that can profitably sell everything it produces attempt to spur output with a plan similar to the one depicted in Figure 3–2? The answer depends on the advantage of the plan relative to alternative ways of increasing productivity, such as adding additional shifts or expanding plant capacity.

These and related questions are difficult but not impossible to answer, and by answering them, you will be able to tailor an incentive program to the unique needs of your organization.

4

Turning Self-Interest Into Teamwork

While the growth of productivity in this country was slowing to a halt, most of us were busy finding reasons to blame OPEC, the federal bureaucracy, and organized labor for our plight. Such blame may be richly deserved. If you take the time to review the facts, however, you will find that the decline in growth of productivity did not occur uniformly. By this I mean that although industry as a whole was fighting a losing battle in the struggle to maintain growth of productivity, an individual firm here or there in that industry was winning. Despite industry-wide declines, these firms were increasing the productivity of their work forces.

These few exceptional organizations and their less productive competitors were operating in the same environment— they paid as much for their energy, complied with the same federal regulations, and dealt with the same unions. Why, then, were they able to run counter to the industry-wide trend? Had these firms discovered secret management techniques that gave them a significant edge on their competitors, or were they merely doing an excellent job of managing with tech-

niques that have been around nearly as long as salt water?
I think the latter was the case. Let me show you what I mean.

HISTORY REPEATS ITSELF

A new category of terms has cropped up in the lexicon of
business. Such names as *productivity circle* and *quality council*
refer to groups of workers and managers who meet regularly
to discuss ways in which the cost and quality of the goods and
services they produce can be improved. In this country, such
groups typically meet on company time. In Japan, evidencing
a different degree of commitment to their organizations, similar
groups normally meet on their own time. In either case, the
practice is a sound one.

Reports of these apparently novel activities have been
abundant in business periodicals and weekly news magazines
in the past few years. Allegedly, these activities constitute
innovative responses to the present, world-wide economic
malaise. In reality, the idea is as old as the hills. Those who
cannot remember the past are condemned to repeat it.[1]

The most noteworthy application of the concepts em-
bodied in productivity circles evolved in the 1930s, as we
emerged from the grips of the Great Depression. This application became known by the name of its notable proponent,
Joseph Scanlon. Most managers probably have heard of the
Scanlon Plan, but relatively few can tell you how it works.
Fewer still have had any direct experience with it, for, according to one survey, as few as 100 firms in the United States are
presently using the Scanlon Plan. Unlike the productivity
council, though, the Scanlon Plan goes beyond encouraging a
few workers to participate in attempts to improve productivity; it provides incentives for all employees—managers and
workers alike—to do so.

[1] Paraphrased from George Santayana's *Birth of Reason*. G. Santayana, *Birth of Reason and Other Essays*, C. Daniel (Ed). New York:
Columbia University Press, 1968.

Desoto, Inc., a manufacturer of paint, is one of the 100-odd companies in the United States that is using the Scanlon Plan today.[2] The company implemented the plan in 1971, at a time when the growth rate of productivity in this country had begun its decline.

Designed to reward employees for increasing labor productivity, the Desoto version of the plan, true to the Scanlon philosophy, was devised as follows: First, a baseline measure of labor productivity was established. For productivity that exceeded the baseline, a bonus was earned, and such earnings were divided between employees (workers and managers, alike) and the company according to a previously agreed-on formula. Second, workers and managers or supervisors in each department of the firm formed production committees to evaluate employee suggestions for improving productivity. Within limits, these committees were authorized to select and implement promising suggestions. Third, managers and elected representatives from the production committees comprised a screening committee that dealt with employee suggestions that were favored by one production committee or another but (1) affected more than one department or (2) required more money to implement than the production committee was authorized to spend.

That's the Scanlon Plan in a nutshell—as simple as one, two, three. There is a host of details still to be considered, but I would like to show you the results and return to the details once you have seen what the plan did for Desoto.

During the first year the plan was in effect, 82 per cent of plant personnel contributed 231 suggestions. Approximately half of these suggestions addressed the problem of improving productivity. The remainder dealt with plant safety and

[2] National Commission on Productivity and Work Quality, *A Plant-Wide Productivity Plan in Action: Three Years of Experience with the Scanlon Plan.* Washington, DC: The National Commission on Productivity and Work Quality, 1975.

grievances. Over the next two years, the proportion of suggestions that directly addressed productivity increased relative to the others. Unfortunately, the study in which these findings are presented provides data only through 1973, and data for subsequent years are not available.

However, the study does report that labor productivity at Desoto increased significantly after the plan was implemented. By 1972 productivity was 28 per cent higher than it had been in 1970, the base year, and by 1973 it had increased 41 per cent.

During the period in question, annual bonuses ranged from about 4 per cent to nearly 11 per cent. The highest monthly bonus achieved in the period was 18 per cent. Yet, because such bonuses resulted from productivity increases, plant output increased while the cost per gallon of paint manufactured declined. Remember that all of this was accomplished at a time when increases in the productivity of labor were tapering off across the nation. All in all, Desoto's efforts seem to have paid off handsomely. With results such as these to demonstrate the potential advantages to be gained from using the Scanlon Plan, why have so few firms adopted it? Why doesn't your firm use it?

Part of management's reluctance to use such techniques may be founded on uncertainty; there can be unanticipated problems associated with unfamiliar systems of management. I will discuss some of these problems later. Another part of management's reluctance to use the plan, though, stems from the amount of effort required to implement such techniques and to manage them effectively. For example, the Scanlon Plan involves the entire organization and requires careful planning and constant participation. Even before the plan is in place, everyone from production to accounting will have contributed to its development. The reluctance to invest so much energy in the face of unknown payoffs is understandable. But you have seen what the potential payoffs can be. What is needed is a closer look at the investment—the effort required to devise and implement a Scanlon Plan.

The Scanlon Plan is uncomplicated, although, as we have seen with other techniques, it must be tailored to the unique characteristics of each organization using it. Thus, the plan usually is described in general terms rather than as a set of specific steps to be followed or rules to be applied. The intent and basic mechanisms of the plan are as follows:

All employees are paid an incentive bonus on the months in which their aggregate productivity exceeds a specified historical average level of productivity. To help improve productivity throughout the organization, every employee is encouraged to submit suggestions to committees that screen them and recommend the promising ideas for implementation. Workers as well as managers participate as members of such committees.

The incentive bonus is based on a baseline measure of productivity for the entire organization. It is a historical measure of performance, taken from records from a period of the firm's recent past that is considered to have been fairly typical or representative of what the future is likely to bring. Usually, this productivity measure is expressed as the ratio of the value of goods produced in a typical period to the labor costs incurred in that period. The value of goods produced includes the value of the net sales for the period as well as the value of additions to (or reductions of) inventories. Labor costs include salaries and wages as well as fringe benefits for the period. A general statement of the baseline ratio is:

$$\text{Baseline Ratio} = \frac{\text{Market Value of Sales} - \text{Returns} \pm \text{Changes in Inventories}}{\text{Salaries} + \text{Wages} + \text{Fringe Benefits}}$$

The market value of sales, rather than actual sales revenues, is used in the ratio because the intent of the Scanlon Plan is to reward employees for outcomes over which they have some degree of control. Although they can control to some extent the amount of output produced in a period, they cannot control the actual sales revenues derived from their output. For instance, management may decide for one reason or another to reduce existing inventories by selling off some of the excess at substantially reduced prices. If markdowns are large enough, sales revenues for the period may fall below those earned in the baseline period, even though labor productivity is well above average. Using the market value of output (which may be defined as the price of the output before discounts and markdowns) provides a more consistent measure of what labor has produced in the current period. In any event, the baseline ratio is used in the computation of incentive bonuses in the manner illustrated in Table 4–1.

In Table 4–1 we find a hypothetical baseline ratio of four to one; that is, the firm's labor costs in a given period comprise one fourth of the market value of the goods produced in that period. For the month used in the illustration, the firm has produced $1 million worth of goods. Using the baseline ratio of four to one, we find that the company should expect its

Table 4–1
Illustration of Bonus Computation Using the Scanlon Plan

$$\text{Baseline Ratio} = \frac{\text{Market Value of Production}}{\text{Total Payroll}} = \frac{\$1,000,000}{\$250,000} = 4:1$$

Gross sales revenue	$1,250,000
Returns	(50,000)
Net sales	1,200,000
Changes in inventory	(200,000)
Market value of production	1,000,000
Allowed payroll (market value of production ÷ Baseline Ratio)	250,000
Actual payroll + fringe benefits	(200,000)
Bonus pool	50,000
Reserve for deficit months (20%)	(10,000)
Bonus pool to be distributed	40,000
Company's share (25%)	(10,000)
Employees' share (75%)	$30,000

$$\text{Bonus as a Percentage of Payroll} + \text{Fringe Benefits} = \frac{\$30,000}{\$200,000} = 15\%$$

labor costs for the period to have been approximately $250,000. However, the actual cost of labor was less, presumably because of increases in efficiency. The difference between the expected and actual costs of labor constitutes the pool from which bonuses will be paid.

The question arises: What happens in months when actual labor costs exceed the historical average? Do the employees refund a portion of their regular earnings to compensate the firm for their relative inefficiency? Rather than resort to such measures, the firm regularly sets aside a portion of the bonus pool as a contingency fund from which it can be compensated in the event of substandard labor productivity. The balance of this fund periodically is distributed as a bonus to employees, though, and a new balance is struck at the beginning of each new period. The percentage of the bonus pool to be reserved for contingencies and the intervals at which the balance of the contingency fund will be distributed are established in the early planning phases of the plan—usually in cooperation with a union or other representative of the employees.

The bonus pool remaining after such contingency funds have been reserved is divided between the company and its employees according to a previously agreed-on formula. The actual formula used varies from company to company, but it is not uncommon for employees to receive 75 per cent of the pool, with the remainder going to the firm.

The employees' share of the bonus is expressed as a percentage of the period's payroll and fringe benefits, and each employee's compensation for the period, including fringe benefits, is increased by this percentage. In some firms, all employees, from the executive suite to the shop floor, share the bonus pool. In others, certain levels of management and sales personnel may be excluded from the bonus plan because they receive other kinds of incentive earnings. Compensation arrangements must be tailored to the characteristics of the organization using the plan.

What has been described so far is not particularly complicated. However, devising an appropriate baseline ratio is no mean feat. Aside from the implied problem in accounting, numerous difficult questions must be answered before a ratio can be calculated. Should all employees, including clerical personnel, sales representatives, and top management, be covered by the plan? What is the rationale for including or excluding each group? Should separate measures of productivity and, thus, separate baseline ratios be established for each area of the firm? Should transactions that, for the most part, are independent of labor productivity be excluded from the productivity measure? An example of a situation in which this question arises is the case in which some of the products sold by a firm merely are purchased from another manufacturer and resold.

Other problems must be anticipated before the plan is installed, even though they will not arise until after the plan has been in effect for some time. For example, the ratio must be revised from time to time to appropriately reflect increases in the costs of factors of production such as labor and materials. If wage and salary increases are not passed on to customers in the form of higher prices, for example, such increases will be gained at the expense of a systematic reduction in bonuses unless the ratio is revised to reflect increased labor costs. This will occur because the increased labor costs will appear as decreased productivity in the bonus computation. This effect can be observed quite simply by increasing the actual payroll and fringe benefits in Table 4–1 by, say, 10 per cent. The result will be a smaller bonus pool, even though labor productivity in this example has remained unchanged.

At the other extreme, increased materials costs have the effect of overstating labor productivity when these costs are passed on as higher prices. Again, a recalculation of the baseline ratio will be in order. In either case, the rationales for, and method of, such calculations should be understood in advance by workers and managers alike, else there is a risk that individuals affected by such recalculations will perceive them to be unfair and perhaps arbitrary.

These are not trivial problems to solve, and before they

are solved, managers and workers from many parts of the organization will find themselves involved in making difficult decisions and tradeoffs. Nonetheless, most organizations routinely solve more difficult problems than these. What is gained in solving them is an incentive program that has two very attractive characteristics that are missing from the kinds of incentive plans discussed in the previous chapter. First, the Scanlon Plan can involve the entire organization. Second, it can encourage employees at all levels to contribute their knowledge of the firm's operations and their ingenuity to the problem of improving productivity. This second characteristic is of considerable interest to management, as evidenced by recent experiments with productivity circles and similar activities.

Suggestions from the Scanlon Plan

As I indicated in the previous chapter, some employees do not think carefully about their jobs because they have little reason to do so. In most cases, these individuals are not in a position to benefit from their ideas. In a few cases, they might be worse off if management were to implement their suggestions for improvements. The general case is exemplified by something I observed a few years ago in a fabrication plant. One of the firm's assembly lines was being slowed down by a bottleneck in one of the assembly operations. The problem was that it was extremely difficult to perform the assembly operation in question because a part that was attached in the previous operation got in the way of the assembly line operator. An engineer was assigned to study the problem, and his approach was to redesign the part that interfered with the subsequent operation.

After the engineer had spent several unproductive days trying to redesign the part, I learned that the assembly line operators had solved the problem but were keeping their solution to themselves. The solution was so simple that it had been overlooked: The order in which the two parts were assembled could be reversed. Although this solution eventually was divulged by the operators and implemented by management, it was kept a secret for several days. Aside from the fact that the assembly line workers had nothing to gain from sharing their ideas with management (the firm did not have a suggestion award program), they delighted in the fact that they had the answer to a problem that better trained, better paid engineers were unable to solve. Apparently, a first-class gloat is one of the few real pleasures of life on the assembly line.

The situation was better than it might have been, though. Suppose that the workers had been compensated according to an incentive payment plan similar to the ones described in the previous chapter. How might the potential consequences of the situation have been altered? For one thing, the workers might have implemented their idea before management became aware of the bottleneck problem. In doing so, and in keeping their assembly methods secret, they might have gained the wherewithal to improve the relationship between effort and reward. Conversely, by volunteering their solution to the problem they might have precipitated a restudy of the job with a potential consequence of having to work harder for the same amount of incentive award. It is clear that the workers' interests are served by withholding such suggestions from management.

As this illustration shows so clearly, life in organizations often is a win–lose proposition, where one group's gain is another group's loss. An essential goal of the Scanlon Plan is to convert such win–lose situations into win–win propositions in which one party's gain is to everyone's benefit.

Win–lose situations are typified by competition for scarce resources. In the distribution of resources that results from such competition, some contestants may receive more than others do. Moreover, one contestant's gains must be taken from other contestants, because there are not enough resources to satisfy each contestant's demands. The results typically are conflict, mutual distrust, and unwillingness to cooperate, among other things.

Win–win situations are characterized by an expanding pool of resources from which all parties can benefit. One individual's gain is not necessarily achieved at the expense of someone else. Rather, all parties can gain simultaneously as the resource pool increases. Furthermore, cooperation and teamwork may develop between these parties as they look for additional ways to increase the supply of resources to be divided.

It is true that the question of who gets what arises in win–win situations because even though each contestant is able to benefit from the increased resource pool, the extent of each contestant's benefit is subject to negotiation. However, when such negotiations result in equitable benefits for all contestants (that is, benefits that are perceived as being equitable), the interests of contestants should be directed toward increasing the amount of resources they will share.

The Scanlon Plan relies on the production and screening committees to achieve success. Once a formula for dividing the productivity bonus between the firm and its employees has been accepted, all employees potentially benefit from increases in productivity. Material productivity gains can be achieved if employees simply work more diligently, avoiding waste and spending their time more productively.

However, additional gains are possible through improvements in work methods and processes. Production committees are formed in each department to explore the latter approach to increasing productivity. Such committees consist of workers elected by members of their departments and their supervisors or managers. However, in small departments that employ relatively few workers, the production committee may include all departmental personnel.

Each production committee is delegated responsibility for reviewing and screening suggestions that are submitted by departmental personnel. Moreover, these committees have the authority to implement promising suggestions provided that the estimated cost of doing so does not exceed a predetermined amount and that the change to be implemented will not affect other departments. In the event that either of these restrictions is encountered, the suggestion is passed on to the screening committee for the entire plant.

A number of studies have shown that between half to

two thirds of the suggestions received by production committees describe potential ways of increasing productivity. The remainder typically fall into two categories—grievances and suggestions concerning working conditions. Grievances generally are forwarded to the firm's or union's grievance committee. Suggestions for improving working conditions may reflect concerns for plant safety, in which case they are passed on to the appropriate plant official. In other cases, they can be considered and, if appropriate, implemented by the production committee, even though they are not directly related to productivity.

This gets us to an important role of the production committee—namely, involving employees in the suggestion system. This is done by explicitly encouraging employee participation and, more important, by providing employees with timely feedback on their suggestions, involving them in modifying, expanding, or clarifying their proposals, and providing recognition for employees whose suggestions are implemented. In light of my earlier comments on positive reinforcement, it should be apparent that these activities are most effective when they are accomplished without delay and when they are rewarding. Immediate, sincere thanks, a form of positive reinforcement, for submitting a suggestion can increase the likelihood that the individual will contribute further suggestions.

The timely implementation of suggestions is also reinforcing for the individuals or groups who submitted them. At each stage of the process of evaluating, screening, and implementing suggestions, the production and screening committees must take pains to avoid unnecessary delays and to maintain the involvement of the originators of the suggestions. If too much time elapses between the submission of a suggestion and the committee's response, the potential for positive reinforcement will be lost.

When suggestions are not implemented by the production committee or when they are rejected or referred to the screening committee, considerable care must be taken to prevent ill will on the part of their originators. People who submit suggestions usually are convinced of their usefulness. Thus, when their suggestions are not implemented, the originators may feel that their ideas did not get a fair hearing. Even when this is not the case, rejection is implied by the decision not to implement a suggestion. Rejection is a very difficult feeling to take in stride, for it often suggests inadequacy of one sort or another.

For these reasons and to encourage employees to continue to submit suggestions, the rationale for not implementing a suggestion must be explained in a way that leaves its originators feeling positive about the Scanlon Plan and their ability to make useful suggestions in the future. Whenever possible, the production committee should work with employees to modify the suggestion and make practical the suggestions that otherwise would be rejected. Moreover, there can be long-run payoffs for implementing suggestions that only break even or that improve only working conditions, but not productivity, if by doing so the production committee provides reinforcement that will result in further, more useful suggestions. All of this may sound time-consuming, but it need not be so. Research on DeSoto's experience indicates that the production committees devote about 24 manhours a month per plant to their tasks. Generally, each committee meets once a month for 10 minutes to one hour.

The screening committees tend to meet for longer periods of time (from one to two hours per month), but they involve fewer employees and, consequently, take up fewer manhours. In keeping with the spirit of the Scanlon Plan, committees sometimes conduct their business on their own time—in carpools or over lunch. Whatever the time spent in committee work, though, it seems to have paid off for DeSoto, as the ratio of production to labor costs indicates.

By now, you may be wondering about the magnitude of the impact that employee suggestions have had on the firm's performance. According to the DeSoto study, each plant has received suggestions that have had or may have substantial impacts. On balance, however, the effect of the average suggestion is modest. This is to be expected. Few goals in life are achieved by sudden insights or unforeseen breakthroughs. Most accomplishments result from long hours of diligent, thoughtful labor. Such modest insights and breakthroughs as are common do not eliminate the burden of toil. Instead, they improve quality here and save a step there, enhancing performance at the margin. Taken together, such improvements in productivity can make a substantial difference in the competitive position of a firm.

Beyond this, the Scanlon Plan has the potential to produce a number of intangible benefits for the organization. It can make clear to employees the extent to which their efforts, the well-being of the firm, and their own financial well-being are inextricably intertwined. It can promote organization-wide teamwork. It can demonstrate to the employees who serve on committees how management decisions are made. It can stimulate creativity and ingenuity among employees, encourage them to learn more about their jobs and the jobs that others perform, and lead to a more knowledgable, more capable work force.

The Scanlon Plan cannot ensure the firm's profitability. It is quite possible for productivity to increase at the same time that sales decline. If the decline in sales becomes severe enough, the firm may find itself in the position of paying its employees productivity bonuses while it operates in the red. This may not be as bad as it seems, however. First, most employees have no direct influence over their firm's profitability. All they can affect is their own productivity and, to some extent, the productivity of others. Productivity can affect profitability, but increased productivity does not inevitably lead to increased profits.

As we have seen, an incentive program can be effective only if it rewards employees for outcomes over which they have some degree of control. Most employees cannot affect their firm's profitability because profits are determined by supply, demand, and the activities of competitors, among other things. For example, profits may decline because a competitor has introduced a better product, because industry-wide demand has fallen off as a result of an economic downturn, or because a new, unsuccessful product has been launched by the firm. Alternatively, the firm's profitability may increase because it has introduced a product that is superior to those of its competitors, because industry-wide demand has increased, and so on.

The question arises: Should the firm reward all its employees when profits increase and lay some of them off as profits decline? How can a profit-sharing system provide an incentive for employees when the majority of them have so little effect on profitability? The obvious answer is that profit sharing is not a completely rational basis for an incentive system. Given that to be the case, how rational is an incentive system that may pay productivity bonuses while the firm is swelling its inventories with unsold goods? More rational, I think, than the alternative systems because no matter what you do, you pay the same price in the end. As long as you pay, you might as well get as much as you can for your money.

A look at standard business practices will help to illustrate this point. The American construction industry, for example, pays what may seem to be extraordinarily high wages to carpenters, plumbers, and electricians. Yet, the earning potential of these workers is less than it appears to be, for they are hired and laid off as the demand for construction waxes and wanes. Some portion of their hourly wage is an inducement to work in an industry that does not provide steady employment. Similarly, part of the automobile assemblyline worker's paycheck is an inducement to work for a firm with a long history of layoffs.

There is a market for labor in which the forces of supply and demand operate just as they operate in markets for goods and services. An industry that can provide steady work for its employees will pay less to fill a particular position than will a second industry that cannot provide steady jobs. At the extreme, some Japanese firms guarantee their employees what amount to jobs with lifetime tenure. In return, they enjoy a more loyal work force and a lower wage bill. There are many other differences between Japanese and American business, but the point is that the Japanese have demonstrated that guaranteed employment and long-run profitability can go hand in hand.

It is one thing to retain a work force during hard times,

but quite another thing to pay productivity bonuses at the same time. The problem is to decide whether you want to increase productivity or not, because you cannot turn labor productivity on and off as you need it. Techniques such as the Scanlon Plan will not be accepted by workers who have cause to believe that their increased productivity may eventuate in layoffs.

Investing in techniques such as the Scanlon Plan is similar to investing in new manufacturing facilities. That is, although new facilities may permit a higher level of productivity than the outdated ones they replaced, the firm will continue to pay for them through good times and bad. Yet, this is not a sufficient reason to refrain from investing in new technology so long as management believes that it can benefit from the investment in the long run. Similarly, the use of techniques such as the Scanlon Plan can provide long-run increases in the productivity of labor. However, such benefits are not without costs, and these must be borne over the life of the investment. Yet, as I mentioned earlier, traditional labor practices also have costs in the form of wages that, in part, compensate workers for future unemployment. Which is better? My point is that it is better to pay for improved productivity even when it is not needed and to develop a thoughtful, cooperative workforce than it is to pay premium wages for lower productivity and the ability to lay off workers who temporarily are unneeded.

5

The Committed Workers

MOTIVATION WITH A VENGEANCE

Remember Twenty-Mule Team Borax? Well, borax (sodium borate) is still used in soaps, but it has also found uses in agriculture, glassmaking, and atomic power generation. So much had the demand for this chemical grown that by the early 1970s U.S. Borax and Chemical Corporation was having trouble keeping orders filled.[1]

A contract between the International Longshoremen's and Warehousemen's Union and the company was due to expire around this time, and the union must have thought it was in for easy pickings. With demand outpacing the company's ability to produce an adequate supply of borax, it may have seemed that a costly settlement would have been preferred by the company to a strike. The union went into negotiations demanding a 25 per cent pay increase and, among other things, the right to a voice in major company decisions.

Far from being a pushover, management immediately began planning to operate its Boron plant with nonunion per-

[1] T. Alexander, "How the Tenderfeet Toughened Up U.S. Borax," *Fortune*, 1974, vol. 90, no. 6, pp. 158–166.

sonnel. In all, 450 employees were recruited for this assignment. They included supervisors from the Boron plant, but also salesmen, scientists, managers, and clerks from other parts of the company. Their assignment was to operate a facility that normally was run by a staff of 1400. What knowledge and skill these white-collar workers lacked, they would have to learn on the job.

When the strike came, the supervisors and novices moved into the plant where they worked 12-hour shifts and received only four days off for every 18 consecutive days worked. Initially, their work was chaotic, but they gradually learned the ropes and were forged into a team by hard labor, long hours, and the challenge of running the plant. Plant output crept back to its normal level and then surpassed it, eventually reaching an all-time record. During this time, labor productivity rose to two to three times what it had been before the strike.

The strike eventually was settled, but many of the strikers found themselves without jobs after the company learned how few people it took to run the plant. That's one way to increase labor productivity; just run your business with fewer employees. However, my purpose in retelling this story is to illustrate two different points. First, none of us normally works up to capacity. In the case of the Boron plant, untrained white-collar workers found that they could achieve levels of labor productivity 100 to 200 per cent higher than the pre-strike average. However, they had to work like Trojans to do this. As I have said, though, most workers could increase their productivity by at least 50 per cent without undue effort if they chose to do so. Second, there probably is nothing special about these 450 strikebreakers. Under different circumstances, they might have been blue-collar workers, employed in the Boron plant and quite content to get by with a little featherbedding here and some goldbricking there. To what cause, then, shall we attribute their heroic efforts? I think that we must attribute their achievements to the challenges they faced in performing such unfamiliar tasks and to their commitment to keep the plant operating at all costs.

Many, perhaps most, of your employees are committed to the traditional American beliefs in the dignity of work and the intrinsic value of achievement. These workers would achieve more at work if their jobs permitted them to do so. They would welcome challenges, greater responsibilities, and more latitude for discretion in decision making. Collectively, they represent an underutilized resource, for their jobs severely limit the talents and energies they can invest in their work.

The untapped abilities of such individuals can be released by the judicious use of a number of related techniques, of which job enrichment is perhaps the simplest. As frequently is the case, job enrichment became something of a fad, generating much enthusiasm and great hopes in the business community. Perhaps it generated too much enthusiasm, for once the novelty wore off, managers seemed to lose interest in the technique. Yet, job enrichment has been used to good effect with workers as diverse as experimental officers in an R & D lab, maintenance personnel, engineering supervisors, assembly line workers, and keypunch operators. The use of the technique with keypunch operators is one of the simplest, most straightforward applications on record. For this reason, I will review the history of this application to demonstrate the technique and its results.

The Setting

Keypunching probably is one of the most boring jobs one can find today. Typically, we think of assembly line work in this regard, but many white-collar positions rival life on the assembly line for sheer monotony. Day in and day out, operators punch holes into cards. Unlike manuscripts of reports and memos that occasionally provide a typist with interesting information and even office gossip, the information that is punched into cards usually is without meaning for the keypunch operator.

Our story begins in a financial institution where four key-punch operators worked under the supervision of a control clerk.[2] Together, these four employees recorded accounting data from various correspondent banks onto punched cards. The supervisor distributed work to the four operators, checked their output and indicated corrections when necessary, and returned completed work to the respective banks. The key-punch operators merely keypunched the transactions onto cards. In general, the work attitudes and morale of these employees were poor.

The Technique

Job enrichment is an approach to job design that attempts to combine fragmented tasks into meaningful units of work in order to create jobs from which workers can derive feelings of responsibility, accomplishment, and self-esteem. Tasks are grouped vertically. That is, the goal of the redesign effort is to create new jobs that involve employees in all aspects of the work—from planning their tasks to responsibility for their results.

Typically, a supervisor plans the work to be done by subordinates and checks their results, as was true in the case of the control clerk who supervised the four keypunch operators. These supervisory functions are delegated to the workers in typical job enrichment programs. By the same token, sequential work processes that are assigned to different individuals are combined, whenever possible, into a single job, permitting the worker to complete an entire sequence of tasks. For example, the various steps that were used to overhaul water meters, described in Chapter 3, might have been combined into a single job to provide more variety and a greater sense of accomplishment than that experienced by workers

[2] M. E. Douglass, and S. T. Johnson, "Successful Job Enrichment: A Case Example," in W. W. Suojanen, M. J. McDonald, G. L. Swallow, and W. W. Suojanen (Eds.), *Prospectives on Job Enrichment and Productivity.* Atlanta, Ga.: Georgia State University, 1975, pp. 237–244.

who repetitively perform only one step in the process and never completely overhaul a meter.

In applying job enrichment to the keypunch operators' jobs, the following changes were made. First, the control clerk's position was eliminated, and the incumbent clerk was promoted to another supervisory post. Next, each keypunch operator was assigned a group of correspondent banks as "clients." Thus, each operator assumed complete responsibility for the jobs submitted by her client banks. Jobs were scheduled, performed, checked, and returned by the operators, who also maintained routine communication with the banks.

The results of the job redesign were as follows. As the day on which the job enrichment program was to be implemented drew near, the keypunch operators, who had positive attitudes toward the changes during the project's planning stages, suffered a decline in morale. They doubted their wisdom in agreeing to take on additional responsibilities and work. Yet, this phase passed, and the operators' morale improved once the project got under way.

An immediate economic gain was the elimination of the control clerk's position. (I was more than half serious when I mentioned that productivity can be improved by doing the job with fewer employees.) Additional improvements in the productivity of the keypunch operators are outlined in Table 4–2. First, the average rate of absenteeism declined from a baseline rate of 5.4 per cent before the program of job enrichment was implemented to 3.1 per cent two months after the

Table 4–2

Productivity Increases Attributed to a Program
of Job Enrichment for Keypunch Operators

Variable	Before Job Enrichment	Two Months After	Seven Months After
Absenteeism	5.4%	3.1%	1.7%
Error rates	1.3%	0.8%	0.7%
Unit/time productivity	21.1 sec.	17.7 sec.	16.8 sec.
Group completion time	181.9 min.	141.0 min.	148.2 min.

jobs were enriched and to 1.7 per cent seven months later. Second, the average baseline error rate of 1.3 per cent dropped to 0.8 per cent two months after the change and to 0.7 per cent by the time seven months had elapsed.

Unit/time productivity is a measure of performance that had been developed by the bank. Basically, it is an average of the time taken to complete a single transaction. Productivity, as measured in this way, improved throughout the seven-month period following the introduction of job enrichment. Two months after the change, the average time to complete a transaction had declined to 17.7 seconds, from 21.1 seconds. After seven months, the time had been reduced to 16.8 seconds.

A second measure of productivity employed by the bank, group completion time, measures the average total time required to complete an entire set of transactions. Again, productivity improvements were observed according to this measure, which declined from 181.9 minutes to 148.2 minutes seven months later. Such improvements speak well for a technique as simple and potentially inexpensive to use as job enrichment.

HOW JOB ENRICHMENT WORKS

Most of the theories that we work with today are incorrect to one degree or another. This is as true in the fields of physics, medicine, and astronomy as it is in the behavioral sciences. Yet, even invalid theories are extremely useful in a practical sense as well as in the scientific disciplines, for they are not totally incorrect. They often lead to thoughts and actions that would not have been contemplated in their absence.

The science of astronomy provides a good example. The pre-Copernican, Earth-centered view of the Universe, although invalid, gave rise to quite accurate systems of navigation and surveying. Even as Copernicus, Kepler, and Newton gradually changed our view of the Universe, navigation remained wedded to the ancient, far-simpler theory. In fact, when I studied navigation some 20 years ago, the textbook I used began by asking the reader to imagine that the Earth was at the center of the Universe.

I have mentioned this in order to raise an important point. Although we have techniques that can be used to increase the productivity of people at work, we do not have, to my knowledge, any valid theories of motivation. Similar to the pre-Copernican view of the Universe, contemporary theories of human motivation have very limited validity, at best, but they have led to some extremely useful practices.

Job enrichment is a case in point. Although the ideas behind this technique were not new at the time it became popular, they were brought into focus for the business community by a study conducted by Frederic Herzberg and his associates.[3] In this research, Herzberg asked subjects, who were employed as accountants and engineers, to recall and describe the times when they felt exceptionally good or exceptionally bad about their jobs. When these anecdotes were analyzed, it was found that different aspects of work were mentioned, depending on whether the respondents were recalling exceptionally good or bad feelings about their jobs. When recalling very positive job experiences, the subjects tended to mention significantly more often than they mentioned other factors achievement, recognition, responsibility, personal growth, the work itself, and advancement. The other factors, which included supervision, working conditions, company policies, interpersonal relations, status, security, and salary, were mentioned more frequently in connection with negative job experiences than they were when positive experiences were described. These findings led Herzberg to conclude that the first set of factors, which he called *intrinsic factors*, contribute to motivation and job satisfaction when they are present in the work environment. However, job dissatisfaction does not result from their absence. Dissatisfaction is created by poor *extrinsic factors* (supervision, working conditions, and

---

[3] F. Herzberg, B. Mausner, and B. Snyderman, *The Motivation to Work*. New York: Wiley, 1959.

the like). When they are good, however, the extrinsic factors do not lead to feelings of satisfaction.

The Herzberg findings became known as the Two-Factor Theory. The major implication of the theory is that motivation and job satisfaction can be increased by redesigning jobs to incorporate more opportunities for achievement, advancement, recognition, and the like. In other words, the theory suggests that job enrichment inevitably leads to increases in morale and productivity.

The route Herzberg traveled to arrive at his theory is fraught with perils. He began by interviewing subjects to learn what made them feel good and bad about their work. Next, he sifted through their responses looking for patterns, which he found. Finally, he restated these patterned findings as a theory. This may seem to be an entirely reasonable way to conduct research, but it has two serious drawbacks. First, it gets the horse before the cart, so to speak, by permitting the findings to determine the theory. A more conservative approach to science is to derive hypotheses from a theory and subsequently test them empirically to determine whether the evidence supports the hypotheses and, thus, the theory. Because the latter approach attempts to test the theory, it is preferable to the former, which merely proposes a theory as an explanation of research data. This is not a trivial point, as will be demonstrated shortly. The second drawback of the approach used by Herzberg is that it may focus attention on patterned data that lend themselves to misinterpretation or that are essentially meaningless. For example, it has been shown that Democratic presidential candidates tend to be elected to office more frequently than Republican candidates in the election years in which National League baseball teams win the World Series. Another whimsical study has shown that presidential candidates whose surnames end with the letter "n" have a better chance of being elected to office than candidates whose names end with another letter of the alphabet— Truman, Johnson, Nixon, and Reagan, for example. So it goes.

These two observations are coincidental and without apparent meaning. It would be pointless to construct a theory that appeared to explain them. In other cases, such as the research in question, it is also pointless to theorize from data, even when the data seem to be intuitively meaningful, and to let the matter rest with the theory. It should be obvious by now that such an approach is meaningful only when there is an intention to empirically test the theory that was constructed to explain the data.

The Two-Factor Theory ultimately was subjected to a number of empirical tests, not by its proponents, but by other scientists who viewed it with skepticism. It is important to note that, with one exception, these research studies were unable to validate the Two-Factor Theory. The exception was the case in which researchers used Herzberg's methodology rather than alternative methodologies. When data were collected using the kind of interview Herzberg used, the results were comparable to Herzberg's. In the remaining studies that employed other ways of collecting data, inconclusive and sometimes contradictory results were found.

This situation led many scientists to conclude that the data on which the Two-Factor Theory is based are merely the result of a peculiar reaction to the research methodology used by Herzberg. Specifically, it was argued that respondents tend to attribute their positive work experiences to their own actions. Negative experiences are attributed to the actions of others. For example, a respondent may readily accept credit for his or her accomplishments at work but may attribute his or her dissatisfaction with failure or low productivity to poor supervision, inadequate working conditions, or the like. It was argued that the questions used by Herzberg's research predisposed the subjects to respond in predictable, biased ways.

As this criticism was being raised, two other things were happening. First, researchers were pointing out that one can interpret Herzberg's data differently and arrive at conclusions that contradict the Two-Factor Theory. For example, when job factors are ranked according to the frequency with which they are mentioned in reports of dissatisfying job experiences, a number of the so-called intrinsic factors turn up at the top of the list. Second, other studies were producing evidence that

raised serious objections to the theory. For example, it was
found that not all workers want more responsibility, advancement, or more challenging work. Some workers would prefer
simpler jobs to jobs that are enriched. These and other research findings contributed to the weight of evidence under
which the Two-Factor Theory eventually crumbled.

And yet, as I have said, the practice of job enrichment
works. It works because it is based on a theory that seems to
be at least partially accurate in describing the motivation of
a particular segment of the work force. Other, quite different
theories also suggest the potential usefulness of job enrichment and similar practices. These other theories range from
explanations of the acquisition of psychological needs in early
childhood to explanations of differences in individuals' adapta-
tions to differing amounts of cortical stimulation. I find them
all to be extremely interesting. Perhaps you would too. Nevertheless, none of these theories has been validated, nor have
any of the theories that were discussed in previous chapters
been validated.

Although this observation may have a chilling effect on
your enthusiasm, it need not and should not affect you in this
way. Psychologists have yet to devise a valid theory of humor,
and we still have jokes. Physicists do not agree on the basic
structure of subatomic particles, but we still build nuclear
power plants. Physicians do not understand the effects of
aspirin on pain, but still they prescribe it. Education does not
offer truth very often. It does three other things, instead. It
shows us how little we really know for certain, it points the
way to learning a little more, and it illuminates the human
potential for making great progress with a few facts and hand-
ful of half-baked theories. Science enables progress—there can
be no doubt of that—but progress need not await the perfection
of science.

All of this is in the way of an explanation of my position
that we do not really know why techniques such as job enrichment work. We could have looked at a half dozen other
theories instead of the Two-Factor Theory, but these would
have shed no more light on the problem. One theory suggests
that certain individuals develop a psychological need for

achievement. Another tells us that people learn to aspire to different levels of achievement. A third says that some people learn to satisfy their needs for psychological growth through their accomplishments in organizations, but that others apparently do not.

For our purposes, it probably is sufficient simply to observe that, for one reason or another, some people have developed committments to their work, and thus they are predisposed to honor these committments through diligent labor. Some people typically respond positively to techniques such as job enrichment, which open new avenues for discharging commitments to work.

PROS AND CONS

Then again, sometimes even committed employees do not respond to enriched jobs. The first reason for this is that some employees have as much, or more, responsibility than they can handle. For example, over a fifth of the nurses who are subjects in an ongoing and, as yet, unpublished research project report that the amount of responsibility that goes with their jobs is more than they want to have. Two thirds of these subjects report that the amount of responsibility is just about right, and only 12 per cent of the nurses report that they would like to assume additional responsibility. Moreover, a second study that employed the same group of subjects indicates that responsibility is one of the second most frequently mentioned factors when the nurses describe times when they considered quitting or seeking demotion or actually quit their hospital.[4] Responsibility is tied with achievement, hospital policy, and administration for second place. The dubious distinction of first place goes to poor technical supervision. Furthermore, a Herzberg-type study of these same nurses shows responsibility to be a significantly greater source of dissatisfaction than of satisfaction.[5] These nurses, I would argue, would not benefit

[4] R.A. Ullrich, "Herzberg Revisited: Factors in Job Dissatisfaction," *Journal of Nursing Administration*. 1978, vol. 8, no. 10, pp. 19–24.
[5] Ullrich, 1978, op. cit.

from the increases in responsibility and opportunities for achievement that result from job enrichment. If anything, job enrichment would result in increased dissatisfaction and turnover. If people have as much or more responsibility than they can handle, little can be gained from adding to their burdens, and much harm can be done.

A second difficulty encountered in using job enrichment is that it does not readily lend itself to jobs that employ ill-structural technologies. As I have said, job enrichment entails putting together fragmented tasks to form complete jobs— that is, jobs that can provide the job holders with a sense of responsibility and accomplishment. Whether or not this can be done depends, in part, on whether one can identify and assemble all the tasks associated with a meaningful unit of work. This should be possible when the technology is well-structured. For example, assembly line tasks can be grouped into larger benchwork jobs in job enrichment programs. However, if the activities required to complete a unit of work cannot be identified ahead of time and combined in some logical sequence, then job enrichment is implausible. When this is the case, it is more meaningful to think in terms of objectives than it is to dwell on tasks.

MANAGEMENT BY OBJECTIVES

Management by objectives, or MBO, is a technique in which managers and their subordinates mutually determine the subordinates' objectives for the coming period. The subordinates, then, are responsible for meeting these objectives. Their managers are responsibile for meeting the objectives to which they have committed themselves in similar meetings with their own bosses *and* for helping their subordinates to accomplish the subordinates' objectives.[6]

[6] G. S. Odiorne, *Management by Objectives: A System of Managerial Leadership.* New York: Pitman, 1965.

The last point is an important aspect of management that frequently is overlooked. We often pay little attention to what our subordinates are doing until they fail. Then we spread the blame around and hope that it lands on the right people. This kind of thing reminds me of a poem that I have forgotten but would like to remember. The poem was about a general who, after winning a battle, walked across the battlefield to survey the devastation he had wrought on the enemy. The last line of the poem went something like this: " 'That will teach them a lesson,' the general said, as he walked among the dead, looking for the educated."

When an employee is punished for not meeting an objective, the lesson that is learned may have come too late to do any good. The time to teach people lessons is when they are striving to meet their objectives, and the lessons that they need to learn are those that will help them to achieve the objectives.

The other two crucial aspects of MBO are: (1) encouraging employees to participate in establishing their own objectives, and (2) holding them accountable for meeting them. The scientific literature in the field is fairly clear on the position that commitment to an objective is increased when the person who must meet the objective in question has had a voice in stating it. As I have said, though, science often can do no more than approximate the truth. Rather than accept the link between participation and commitment as a fact, we will do better merely to view it as a reasonably good conclusion to draw, given the scientific evidence that is available at present.

The major difference between MBO and job enrichment is that MBO permits the employee much greater freedom to select the means by which an objective will be pursued. Objectives, not tasks, are the employee's responsibilities, which is particularly important when ill-structured technologies are employed—when we are faced with situations in which the next step in the work process will be determined, in part, by the results of the previous steps.

Beyond this, MBO involves the employee in setting objectives. Moreover, when properly managed, the technique focuses management's attention on the need to monitor subordinates' progress and to provide them with necessary help when they need it. The old management principle that holds that authority can be delegated but responsibility cannot applies very well here. Under MBO, management ultimately is responsible for seeing that subordinates meet their objectives. What can result is a system of management in which the boss becomes the person who helps those at lower levels of the organization to achieve success. When subordinates become aware of this, they may realize that it is better to ask their supervisors for help as soon as they need it than it is to wait until things have gone completely wrong. When the employees reach this awareness, they and their supervisor become a team whose job it is to achieve the goals they have agreed to meet.

Evaluation and rewards, whether monetary or in the form of praise, are based on the period's objectives. In a sense, this is similar to both positive reinforcement and the incentive systems that have been discussed in previous chapters. Clearly stated objectives, feedback on performance, and reinforcement for work that accomplishes these objectives are familiar concepts by now. What MBO does in addition is to provide responsibility, opportunities for achievement, and the potential for growth—aspects of work to which the committed worker will respond.

THE PROBLEM OF UNCERTAINTY

It seems that no management technique has generated more horror stories than MBO. Sometimes I am even reluctant to talk to managers about MBO because in a group of 10 managers at least one, it seems, will have a story to tell about how badly things went when his or her firm tried to use it.

The reasons for these disappointing experiences are not difficult to understand. In some cases, MBO simply has been poorly managed. I know of cases, for example, in which managers simply did not attempt to help their subordinates meet their objectives. In other cases, managers failed to reward subordinates according to their success in meeting objectives. Rather, they gave the biggest salary increases to their friends, regardless of how well they had performed vis-à-vis their objectives. You can imagine the impact that such practices can have on the motivation of other employees.

Other occasions of failure provide a more serious topic for study because they are not caused merely by ineptitude or ill will. These occasions are typified by situations in which the subordinate's objectives change at so great a pace that the objectives established at the beginning of a period bear little relationship to the actual objectives accomplished within the period. When this happens, MBO cannot work. Why does it happen? It is most likely to happen when we are unable to specify with a reasonable degree of certainty the sequence of steps that will result in the achievement of an objective— that is, when the technology we are using is ill-structured. If your subordinates are performing the steps that will contribute to some larger objective, and if these steps (which are the subordinates' objectives) can change drastically as work toward the objective progresses, then a system such as MBO probably will be inappropriate.

MBO may be inappropriate for still another reason. Employees and managers alike may not know how to go about achieving an objective. Techniques that can be used to increase productivity in cases such as these are the subject of the next chapter.

6

From Commitment
to Achievement

SUPPORTING PRODUCTIVITY

What do you make of the fact that only 12 per cent of the nurses mentioned in Chapter 5 reported that they aspired to greater responsibilities? Are the other 88 per cent without ambition and content to accomplish no more tomorrow than they did today? How should the hospital's administration interpret such data?

The interpretation that emerged from the study was straightforward but melancholy. One nurse reported that she had been assigned to temporary duty in the hospital's intensive care unit. She claimed that she lacked both prior experience and adequate training in intensive care nursing and was not competent to carry out the responsibilities that she had been assigned. Another reported being on duty in the emergency room when numerous victims of an automobile accident were brought in. Some of the injured were in grave condition. The emergency room staff did their best, she said, but they could not provide medical care as quickly as it was needed. There were barely enough skilled hands in the emergency room that day to meet the needs of the injured. A third nurse was convinced that the treatment that had been prescribed for her patient was not only incorrect but potentially harmful. She was on a night shift. The attending physician could not be reached for some reason or other. Rumor had it that he occasionally left his paging device at home when he went out, so as not to be disturbed. The nurse lacked the authority either to change the prescription or to refuse to administer it.

In these three cases and in others the subjects of the study reported that they felt responsible for the well-being of their patients, but that they were more or less helpless to discharge these responsibilities adequately. This seems to explain why the majority of the nurses studied do not want additional responsibilities, and why a substantial minority of them actually would prefer to have fewer responsibilities. They are not lazy or without ambition. Rather, they are burdened with responsibilities that neither you nor I would want to share.

The reports provided by these nurses are exceptional; they do not portray normal events in the hospital. Yet, they do illustrate dramatically the essence of more commonplace events in which employees labor under responsibilities that they cannot shoulder. As a commonplace example, consider a group of sales representatives who have been told by their manager to increase their volume of sales. Their objective is clear enough, but how shall they accomplish it? If they knew how to close more sales, they most likely would already be selling more than they do.

Selling is an activity that employs an ill-structured technology. The goal of personal selling is to influence the behavior of customers. Some activities that can influence behavior lend themselves to well-structured technologies. For example, positive reinforcement, as described in Chapter 1, uses a logical sequence of steps that have fairly predictable consequences. Unfortunately, the technique, which can be used to influence employees to begin work in time or to avoid accidents, is not as useful in more complex situations, such as one in which a potential customer is influenced to purchase an information-processing system or an insurance policy. How, then, can our sales representatives be helped to accomplish the objectives set by their manager?

SYSTEM FOUR

By the 1960s Rensis Likert's term, *System Four Management*, had become a byword in industry.[1] Likert had categorized management by four basic types. System One is an exploitative, authoritarian approach to managing people. System Two stands for a more benevolent form of authoritarianism, the type exemplified by my high school principal, as I remember. According to Likert's scheme, System Three is a philosophy of management that fosters consultation with subordinates—an approach that advocates listening to the opinions of others and using them wherever it is practical to do so, but that acknowledges management's exclusive right to make decisions, nonetheless. Conversely, System Four management advocates the participation of subordinates in decisions that affect them.

Likert's research included studies that had members of departments in various organizations describe their departments according to these four categories of management. A fairly elaborate questionnaire was used for this purpose. One result of this research was the finding that the highest producing departments studied were described as being more or less like System Four. The lowest producing departments invariably were described by respondents as being similar to Systems One and Two.

A closer look at System Four management is instructive. System Four is based on three concepts: (1) supportive relationships among all members of the business unit, (2) high performance goals, and (3) a commitment to group decision making and supervision. The first two concepts are familiar from our discussion of MBO, in which management's respon-

[1] R. Likert, *The Human Organization: Its Management and Value.* New York: McGraw-Hill, 1967.

sibilities include encouraging the establishment of high performance standards and supporting subordinates in their
attempts to meet them. The concept of group decision making
and supervision has not arisen in previous discussions of other
techniques, however. An example will illustrate what Likert
had in mind.

One of Likert's studies compared 20 high-producing
sales units with an equal number of low-producing units of a
large sales organization. As you might suspect, given the drift
of this chapter, the managers of the high-producing units
advocated high performance goals and supported their sales
representatives in their efforts to achieve these goals. In the
less successful sales units, managers supported their employees,
but they did not encourage high standards of achievement,
or they set high standards but were not supportive, or they
did neither.

Moreover, the high-producing units invariably adopted a
form of group decision making and supervision. For example,
the sales representatives in such units regularly met as a group
with their manager to review their performance, to advise one
another on ways to improve performance, and to set sales
goals for themselves. It is important to note that the manager's
function in these meetings was to help subordinates to set
objectives and to meet them, and not to judge them or tell
them what they must achieve.

In a typical meeting, each sales representative reviewed
his or her performance by recounting, among other things, the
prospective customers identified during the previous period,
the number of sales calls made, the kinds of presentations
employed, the closings attempted, and the results of these
efforts. Other sales representatives would then discuss the
activities described, offering suggestions and advice for improving the next period's sales. Finally, the sales representative
in question, with the advice of the manager and other sales
persons, would establish a goal for the next period.

As simple as it sounds, the System Four approach produces good results according to Likert's data. Its potential for success in the kind of situation described previously can be attributed to a number of factors. First, it provides a way of helping people who are confronted with problems that cannot be solved by well-structured technologies. Lacking the rules, formulas, and programs for problem solving that typify well-structured technologies, the individual must rely on insights, hunches, trial-and-error techniques, judgment, and the like. A group of co-workers who have confronted and solved similar problems constitutes a rich source of approaches to such ill-structured problems. Help of this sort can equip the individual to face responsibilities that otherwise he or she would not know how to meet.

Second, the process of group problem solving and supervision is similar in some respects to the Scanlon Plan. Specifically, it transforms what otherwise might be a win–lose situation into a win–win proposition. The sales representatives in the preceding example were encouraged to help one another to become successful rather than to compete directly with one another. Competition within an organization often precludes cooperation among the competitors. In a sense, one person's success in a competitive situation is measured relative to the failures of others. However, when each individual's success is measured relative to a goal he or she has established, then all members can succeed. What is more, an individual's accomplishment, as determined under System Four management, includes his or her success in helping co-workers to achieve their goals. Thus, for anyone to succeed as a sales representative in this example, others must have been helped to succeed as well.

System Four management provides unique opportunities for achievement, responsibility, and the like that are not available through either job enrichment or, in most cases, MBO. Under System Four, each employee can become an informal trainer, consultant, and problem solver for the group. Beyond being an outstanding sales representative, for example, an experienced individual can take pride in having helped develop the next generation of employees. Among other things, such experience in employee development is invaluable training for future positions in management.

When System Four is used as Likert advocates, each sales manager belongs to a second group that is similar to the ones that comprise the managers and their sales representatives. The second group consists of all sales managers and their immediate superior. These higher level groups function in much the same way as do the groups previously described. That is, the managers review with their colleagues and superior their performance relative to the last period's goals, discuss potential means for improving their units' performance, and set new goals for the coming period.

The managers' immediate superior belongs to a third group that comprises other superiors and their boss. This pattern of overlapping group membership is repeated, in some cases, until everyone from the chief executive officer to the janitor is included in at least one group. Each member of the organization, except the chief executive officer and the janitor, plays a linking-pin role; groups at different levels of the organization are linked by members who belong to contiguous groups. Together, the individuals who belong to two organizational groups constitute an informal network for communicating upward and downward in the hierarchy.

All of this may seem quite elaborate; it requires major changes across the entire organization. Yet, System Four management can be effective even when it is applied to a single unit or department. Given a reasonable amount of commitment on the part of subordinates, you might consider using System Four in just one unit of the organization before advocating its use elsewhere. Its acceptance by other parts of the organization can be enhanced if its success in a pilot application can be demonstrated.

Moreover, a pilot application will illustrate some of the problems that can be encountered in using System Four and can provide valuable experience in handling them. A major difficulty is that managers and supervisors sometimes lack the leadership skills that are required by the technique. Rather than giving orders and monitoring performance, managers who use System Four find themselves trying to help their subordinates formulate reasonable objectives, evaluate their own performance, and counsel others. And they must accomplish these things while emphasizing to the group the relationships their objectives must bear to those of the organization. Managers who have led project teams, task forces, and the like will have experienced demands similar to those made of management by System Four. Others may need advice, encouragement, and sometimes even training before they can use the technique effectively.

These and related problems can be mastered ultimately. A more serious problem is the possibility that the groups may operate without adequate information. For example, in the case of the sales organization, how can the sales representatives judge the adequacy of their objectives except in the light of their past performance?

SURVEY FEEDBACK

A second, related technique remedies the potential shortcoming (inadequate information) of System Four, which can pose serious problems in certain applications. The Survey Feedback technique relies on overlapping groups that are similar to those used by System Four, but in addition, such groups routinely are provided relevant information tailored to their needs. To use the same example, branch sales managers receive periodic reports of company sales, branch sales, and the sales of departments within their respective branches. Department managers receive sales reports for their respective branch, for all departments within their branch, and for each of the sales units within their department. Unit managers, in turn, are provided sales reports for their respective departments, for each unit within their department, and for all sales representatives within their unit. Each group in the organization is provided information in a form that is potentially useful in solving that group's problems.

As for the rest, the Survey Feedback technique operates the same way that System Four does. Each group meets periodically to discuss the implications of the data, to propose new courses of action that are derived in part from these data, and to assist one another in implementing these courses of action.

The reason for using sales information in this example is obvious. However, many other kinds of data can be used as well. Data on competitive activity, employee turnover, selling expenses, new market developments, product defects, and the like can be distributed to the groups for their attention, recommendations, and action.

Several aspects of this technique indicate its potential value to the organizations that use it. First, the overlapping groups provide an established network for two-way communication in the organization. Ideas and suggestions that are developed in a group can be passed upward or downward, as appropriate, to the level of the organization that has the authority to evaluate and implement them. Typically, numerous ideas developed by lower level personnel are passed upward for management's consideration. Communications upward and downward are facilitated by the linking-pin members of the groups.

Second, the technique gets information to the levels of the organization where it can be used. Branch managers in our example cannot effectively use data on the performance of individual sales representatives, but they can make use of information that compares the performance of departments within their respective branches. Sales unit managers, though, need comparative data on the performance of their sales representatives, but probably they would benefit little from having data on the performance of the firm's various branches.

Third, collecting and distributing data throughout the organization can establish a degree of objectivity that frequently is lacking in organizations. Many of the organizations with which I work create and live by their own myths. They tend to declare much of what they do to be successful, without trying to determine whether this actually is the case. Consequently, they ignore much of what they are doing poorly. These organizations watch some aspects of their performance like hawks and they place great emphasis on improving them, but they also tend toward blindness when it comes to other important facets of the organization.

There are a number of reasons for this attitude. All managers are encouraged to look good in the eyes of their superiors. Consequently, they tend to emphasize the success of their operations and to minimize or even obscure their deficiencies. In most organizations, they would be ill-advised to do otherwise. Next, among the norms that influence behavior in organizations is the typical belief that employees should be enthusiastic, positive, and supportive. The manager who constantly finds fault and points out needed improvements is likely to be considered as an "attitude problem." The insidious predicament of the critic is that fault finding implies criticism of bosses and colleagues who, after all, would surely know if things weren't up to par. Then again, some organizations neglect to collect data that would objectively describe problems and opportunities. To compound these problems, many organizations have learned to live with problems and, consequently, to ignore them, even though solutions to the problems exist. One department of a hospital, for example, does a poor job of financial planning because it lacks the talent and time to do any better. Meanwhile, another department in the same organization is using a computerized financial planning model with good results. Top management has rejected the second department's offer to make its model available to other units in the organization because, "Our accounting department has all the software it needs."

The use of data in the Survey Feedback technique does not guarantee that all problems will be solved or even identified. However, it does have the tendency to shatter organizational myths and to raise questions such as: "Why is department

A so far ahead of the other departments in this regard, and why is turnover so high in Department C?" It substitutes comparative data for unfounded opinions, and it can identify opportunities as well as problems.

The Survey Feedback technique does several other things. It attempts to solve problems at the places where they occur in the organization. For example, if Department D's labor turnover rate is found to be significantly higher than the average for other departments, the place to begin looking for the problem is in the department itself. The members of Department D, including their supervisor, probably are in a better position to identify the causes of this problem and its potential remedy than are managers in other remote parts of the organization. Moreover, the people experiencing the problem may be more motivated to solve it than are others, who have other fish to fry. Then again, the members of the department will be more likely to accept a solution to which they have contributed than a solution that is imposed on them by some other part of the organization. They will be in a better position to implement it as well. Because they have worked with the solution, they will understand it better than they would a solution developed by another group.

According to Floyd Mann, one of the original proponents of the Survey Feedback technique, the use of survey data as a vehicle for organizational change is more compatible with the culture of contemporary organizations than are numerous other change techniques.[2] The use of survey data and the emphasis on problem solving are familiar aspects of managerial work. Thus, they are not as likely to be rejected as are other, more behaviorally oriented techniques. In addition, the survey data lend an air of objectivity to discussions of performance that otherwise could become quite emotional.

A word of caution is in order here. The appearance of objectivity does not necessarily imply the objectivity, accuracy,

[2] F. C. Mann, "Studying and Creating Change: a Means to Understanding Social Organization," in C. M. Arensberg et al. (eds.). *Research in Industrial Human Relations.* New York: Harper, 1957, pp. 146–167.

or validity of the data. Although we are all aware of some of the limitations of accounting data, the limitations of other kinds of data on organizational performance have never been made quite as explicit. For example, I have never been convinced that employee satisfaction should be measured with a linear scale, that there is a high correlation between what people actually feel and what they indicate on satisfaction scales, or that there is much of a relationship between satisfaction as reported on these scales and performance on the job. My advice here is the same as it was in Chapter 1: Whenever you can, look at outcomes rather than hypothetical constructs. I do not mean that management should be indifferent to the satisfaction or dissatisfaction of other members of the organization. However, merely conducting an attitude survey will do little to improve anyone's lot in the organization, except perhaps provide an interesting job for someone in the personnel department. It would be better, in my opinion, to ascertain that people have challenging work to accomplish if they want it; that employees are provided the resources, including the assistance and support of management, to adequately discharge the responsibilities they have been given; that rewards are commensurate with contributions to the organization; that problems that are obvious to other people in the organization are also recognized by management; and so on. Doing these things probably will contribute more to the morale of your organization than will all of the concern for employee satisfaction that you can muster on a good day.

7

Using Consultants Effectively

SEAGULLS AND OTHER NONSENSE

A few years back, I had a brief and unproductive telephone conversation with a manager who wanted to know whether I would give a talk for his organization on *Johnathan Livingston Seagull*. In case you missed this one, *Johnathan Livingston Seagull* was a novel about a seagull who entered a realm of higher consciousness—a sort of Zen marsh bird. It seemed that the manager had been quite impressed by a discussion of J.L.S. that had been part of a management development program he had attended in California. You know how they are in California.

This occurred in the early 1970s, at a time when there were more communes than colleges in the United States; when logic and rationality were seen as character defects by the advocates of sensate science; and when it seemed that half of the country had forsaken standard English in favor of encounter-group Creole. The philosopher, Max Black, may have seen all this coming in the late 1940s when he wrote, with tongue in cheek, "In any matter of serious concern, you will *feel* strongly that a certain conclusion *must* be right. This is the clue to success in really sound thinking. Let yourself go—think in technicolor." Well, all that has changed—or has it? Last spring, I was asked to give a talk entitled, "Spring Cleaning Your Workers' Attitudes." For the love of Pete!

Other than the fact that one topic was a bit more bizarre than the other, both managers were evidencing essentially the same shortcoming. Neither one seemed to have been concerned with the possibility that his firm may have had problems, or with the possibility that a talk on seagulls or employee attitudes might have done nothing at all to address these problems. Moreover, this shortcoming seems to be fairly widespread. Other callers ask, "Do you do transactional analysis, assertiveness training, management in the '80's . . . ?" So it goes.

It might be argued that a three-day seminar on just about any topic that is even remotely relevant to management will do some good, even if it is not addressed to a specific problem that the firm is experiencing. This argument ignores three crucial points, however. First, seminars by themselves do not solve organizational problems. They can provide information, to be sure, but we are already bombarded by information that we have neither the intention nor the opportunity to use. For educational activities to lead to improvements in an organization, they should be tailored to the kinds of changes that management intends to make; they should be designed in conjunction with a program of change to which the organization is committed. Otherwise, the ideas that are presented probably will not find their way into practice. Second, seminar participants typically are not held accountable by their employers for their performance as participants. This situation could be improved if employees routinely were provided opportunities to demonstrate their ability to make effective use of the information learned in seminars. Such opportunities could range from demonstrations of direct applications of knowledge to proposals to management for organizational improvements that are based on this knowledge. Finally, there is the problem that some seminars, such as the one on the fabled Johnathan Livingston Seagull, have little to contribute to organizational performance. For example, although millions of dollars have been spent by business organizations on sensitivity training over the past 20-odd years, no scientist has been able to demonstrate acceptable evidence of a relationship between sensitivity training and such outcomes as increased productivity or profitability. What is worse, a major study of the effects of T–groups conducted by Lieberman and his associates eventually found that the casualty rate (the rate of occurrence of enduring negative psychological reactions) in such groups approaches 10 per cent—a rate that, to the authors, ". . . is alarming and unacceptable in an endeavor calculated to foster positive growth." [1]

Be that as it may, not many firms are buying T–groups today. Instead, they are sending participants to seminars on assertiveness training, leadership skills, time management, fundamentals of this, and how to do that. There are better ways to spend money, and there are more productive ways to use consultants.

A RETURN ON INVESTMENT

What does your organization spend on consulting and management development? What are the financial returns to the organization from these expenditures? These questions may sound odd coming from an academician, but they shouldn't. In my work, I must value knowledge for its own sake. In your work, knowledge is a means to an end. Before you invest in knowledge, you ought to know how you will use it and how your organization will benefit from its use. If you can use expert advice to solve a problem, and if a solution to the problem is worth at least as much as the cost of such advice, then you will want to buy the best advice you can find. If not, you may as well save your money.

All organizations have problems, and many of them can

[1] M. A. Lieberman, I. D. Yalom, and M. B. Miles, *Encounter Groups: First Facts*. New York: Basic Books, 1973. p. 193.

be solved fairly easily. Often, however, these problems go unnoticed until they become serious. When this happens, an outsider—a new manager or a consultant—is likely to arrive on the scene, and what the newcomer typically does is what management should have been doing all along. The outsider identifies the organization's major problems and attempts to correct them.

One of the on-going responsibilities of management is problem finding, that is, looking for overlooked problems and opportunities in the organization. It generally is quite easy to find problems and opportunities. The process begins with asking questions. How productive are our employees? What will our personnel requirements be in six months? What is our rate of labor turnover? Why do people leave the organization? What is the competition doing about this? Is this the way we should be organized? What should I be doing for customers that I am not doing now?

Although preliminary answers to these questions may come to mind, such questions cannot be answered adequately without empirical information. Thus, the next step is to collect data from individuals and company records that will either support or disconfirm whatever your preliminary answer might have been. When you start digging up the facts, you may find that things are not quite as peachy as you had assumed them to be.

There are a number of ways to state a problem, but only one of them is productive. For example, suppose that absenteeism in your shop is significantly above the average for previous years. You could define the problem to be that absenteeism is high because employees have poor attitudes toward work these days, but if you define the problem this way you probably will not be able to solve it. After all, there is very little that you can do about the public's attitudes toward work. Moreover, poor attitudes may not be the cause of the problem; they merely may be correlated with absenteeism. Alternately, they may have no relationship to absenteeism at all. Second, you could define the problem more elegantly and simply say that absenteeism is too high. It would be much

better, though, to define the problem to be to reduce absenteeism from its present level of X shifts per hundred to
$(X - N)$ shifts per hundred. There are advantages to stating a
problem this way. First, the problem is couched in terms of
an objective to be met. Since this must be done sooner or
later, if the problem is to be solved, it is better to do it at the
outset, least the objective get lost in the shuffle. Second, the
statement of the problem is free of conjecture about its causes.
Such causes should be determined empirically, after the problem has been stated. Stating the problem in terms of hypothetical causes can lead to wasted effort as attempts are made
to alter conditions that, in actuality, do not bear on the
problem.

At this point, it will pay to estimate the value of a solution
to the problem. How much would the firm save if it actually
reduced absenteeism from X to $(X - N)$? What would be the
returns if productivity in Department A was increased by 2
per cent? In some cases, estimated benefits are difficult to
obtain. Yet, when they can be made they provide a measure
of the relative importance of the various problems that have
been identified. Moreover, they suggest the upper limits of
what management should be willing to spend on their solutions. Thus, they provide a way to estimate the return that
can be expected from an investment in a solution.

ON SELECTING CONSULTANTS

The investigation of the problem may suggest one of the
techniques discussed in previous chapters as a potential remedy.
Alternatively, another type of organizational change may
seem appropriate—a change in production methods, materials,
or accounting procedures, for example. Be that as it may,
other organizations or other departments in your own organization may have dealt successfully with similar problems.
Therefore, you may want to raise the problem informally
with your counterparts and colleagues. Who knows, if they

have not solved the problem, perhaps they have it too. You might also raise the problem with a consultant at this point. The right consultant for your purposes should be able to describe the procedures used by other organizations to solve similar problems and be able to document the results of these efforts. Ordinarily, a consultant will not be able to do this off the cuff, but the one you are looking for should be able to do it after studying the problem. The point is that if the consultant cannot do this, you ought to have second thoughts about the return that you can expect to realize from your investment in consulting services.

I do not mean to suggest that there are pat solutions for all organizational problems. Many problems are ill-structured, and their solutions, if they can be found, are shaped and modified by experience. Yet, I do want to emphasize the point that a consultant should be able to describe solutions to similar ill-structured problems that have been employed in other organizations, as well as the differences among these solutions and the major reasons for such differences.

There undoubtedly are problems for which adequate solutions have never been found. Such problems sometimes lend themselves to research. However, there are major qualitative differences between consulting and research. It is worthwhile to raise particularly vexing problems with scientists or scholars who often are well-versed in the research literature dealing with your particular problem and who consequently will be able to tell you whether or not enough is known about the problem to solve it. In the event that the problem lies in an area of interest to science, you may find the tables turned, so to speak. For many researchers, the opportunities to study problems of interest are limited. Such individuals will welcome a chance to collect data in your organization and to share with you their results. This has potential advantages and disadvantages. On the one hand, researchers normally do not charge fees. On the other, they cannot guarantee that their results will be meaningful or immediately useful. However, when solutions do not exist, research offers at least the possibility of a better understanding of the problem. Such understanding eventually may lead to solutions. In any event, there is little need to pay a consultant for services that a scientist feels morally committed to provide.

ON USING CONSULTANTS

Most management consulting activity is in two areas—training and problem solving. The separation of these consulting activities is unfortunate, and in my opinion it has often resulted in poor returns on the resources invested in such consulting services. I have suggested the basis for this opinion and will dwell somewhat further on it. I will conclude by proposing steps that can be taken to reduce the degree of separation and, thereby, to permit a more effective use of consulting services.

Management training closely parallels post-secondary business education in terms of its form and substance. Seminars, lectures, and case discussions have survived being transplanted from university to firm and have thrived, as have the theories and constructs of management. The use of higher education as a model for management development was predictable and understandable. It may have been unfortunate, as well.

Although it faltered somewhat in the 1960s, America's faith in higher education has been enduring. Yet, such faith in education, similar to faith in the judicial system, often is uninformed. The missions and methods of higher education generally are not well understood, and consequently there are confusion and occasionally disappointment regarding the product of the educational system. There is also the false expectation that the means employed in higher education are appropriate for doing things that, in fact, they were never meant to do.

The mission of higher education hardly has changed since antiquity. It is ". . . the preservation of the eternal truths, the creation of new knowledge, and the improvement of service wherever truth and knowledge of high order may serve the needs of man." [2] Teaching is a vehicle for the preservation of truth and knowledge across the generations. It is also one of the ways in which the university attempts to improve its service to society. Yet, not all educators strive to achieve both these goals in their teaching. In schools of agriculture, law, management, and medicine they usually do, but in undergraduate programs in astronomy, English, history, and physics they often do not. The departments that teach the humanities and sciences as undergraduate majors have educational, not vocational, missions. It is not a goal of these baccalaureate programs to train astronomers, Shakespearean scholars, or historians. Only the doctoral programs taught in these areas train them. Nonetheless, many college students and their parents are dismayed to find that their undergraduate educations in the nonprofessional fields have not equipped them with entry-level work skills.

The professional schools, such as schools of management, are concerned with the advancement of knowledge, with imparting knowledge for its own sake, but they are also concerned with training students to use some of this knowledge in their future jobs. Yet, the vocational aspect of professional education receives the least emphasis because the professional schools (or at least the better ones) remain faithful to the scholarly, scientific, and educational goals of the larger university. As a result, theory is taught at the expense of entry-level job skills, and the intellectual accomplishments of students, rather than their entrepreneurial achievements, are admired and rewarded. Most of a professional student's vocational training takes place outside of the laboratory and classroom, after formal academic requirements have been met. It takes place in clerkships for law graduates, in student-teaching programs for education majors, in internships for doctors, and in on-the-job training programs for graduates of business schools. Unfortunately, this point seems to have been overlooked in management development programs.

[2] C. Kerr, *The Uses of the University.* Cambridge, Mass.: Harvard University Press, 1963, p. 38.

It is not difficult to understand why management training programs have emulated post-secondary education. For one thing, few other educational models are known well enough to have been copied. For another, the university's educational practices are shrouded in status. The status of participants in graduate seminars is also felt by those who are fortunate enough to attend management development seminars.

Nevertheless, university seminars, lectures, and discussions are intended to educate participants; they are not designed to impart vocational skills. Such skills are mastered after the lectures and seminars have ended, when the students attempt to solve problems by applying the knowledge that they have gained. Skills of any sort are mastered only as they are practiced.

Organizations may use management training activities merely to educate their personnel. This is a noble and sometimes practical goal. However, it probably is a mistake to assume that management seminars alone lead to material improvements in organizational performance. For performance to improve, knowledge must be increased, skills in using this knowledge must be developed or enhanced, and opportunities to apply newly acquired skills and knowledge to organizational problems must be provided. Only the first of these three essential conditions is produced in the usual approach to management development.

This problem is not overlooked, to be sure. Cases, simulations, and similar exercises are used by universities and management development programs alike to foster development of skills. These surrogates for managerial problem-solving experience may be the best that we can provide for inexperienced 19- and 20-year-old undergraduate business majors. However, they are poor approximations of the actual experience and are unnecessary in management development programs whose participants live in a workaday world that is rich in problems to be solved and opportunities to practice skills.

The key to combining education with development of skill so that improved organizational performance results is to view performance—not education—as the essential concern of management development activities. One implication of this shift in emphasis is that management development activities should take place in response to a demand that arises from the identification of problems the organization cannot solve because it lacks crucial knowledge and managerial skills. In other words, organizations would do better to employ the services of management educators when they need these services to solve problems than they do by routinely sending their personnel to "off-the-shelf" seminars.

A second implication is that management development programs should be tailored to address specific problems identified by management and to examine these problems within the context of a particular organization. I have tried to emphasize the point that each of the solutions to organizational problems that is described in the preceding chapters was modified to "fit" the organization in question. To the extent that management development becomes a step in the process of solving problems, it too must be modified.

A third, related implication is that management development and research on organizational functioning should merge. If training programs are to be focused on specific problems of the organization, then data describing these problems should be gathered and used in the seminar. In other words, baseline and other data that are relevant to the problem in question should be included in the information presented in management development programs.

The final and major implication to be discussed here is that management development programs should result in improved organizational performance—in solutions to the problems from which the demand for management development emerged. Moreover, the actual experience of the individuals who are involved in solving these problems should become the substance of further management development efforts. The reason for this is quite simple. Suppose that an organization hires a management development staff to improve the archery scores of its personnel. After a few lectures on archery techniques, the employees are led to a target range to practice with bows and arrows. Individuals' scores tend to improve somewhat after a few practice sessions, but relatively few become proficient as archers. Why? Because some people are not standing as they were instructed to stand before the target. Others are not releasing the bow string correctly. One employee closes his eyes before he fires for unknown reasons. Is this not what you would expect? What is needed is further instruction in which each archer's performance is observed and corrected by the trainer.

Similarly, after employees have been taught what they need to know in order to solve a particular problem, they must be provided with opportunities to apply this knowledge. Next, their efforts must be examined in light of both the results they are achieving and the extent to which they have conformed to the procedures required by the technique that they are trying to use. Further instruction, as well as reinforcement for their accomplishments, will be needed by these employees in most cases. Obviously, the management development consultant will be in a position to provide advice, encouragement, and reinforcement. However, the employees' peers will be able to provide these things as well, and what may result is a situation akin to System Four or Survey Feedback in which the employees and the consultant become a problem-solving team. This cycle of performance, feedback, evaluation, correction, and reinforcement will be enhanced to the extent that it is formally structured—that is, made an integral part of the management development program.

This is the crux of the argument, but there are a few other points to be added. First, there are some occasions when an organization cannot justify learning to do for itself what the consultant can do for the organization. Such occasions typically arise when the organization must solve a nonrecurring (or infrequently occurring) problem such as site planning. On most occasions, however, organizations have continuing needs for the consultant's skills. Such occasions typically end in one of several ways. Frequently, the organization finds that it lacks the skills that are needed to implement changes advocated by the consultant. When this has been the case, countless proposals from consultants have been received, paid for, and placed on shelves where they gather dust. Alternatively, some organizations retain the consultant's services in order to implement the proposed changes. The result is that the organization tends to become dependent on the consultant for the skills it needs but does not have. Finally, the organization may attempt to learn the consultant's skills so that it will be equipped to implement changes on its own. This is the most desirable outcome of client–consultant relationships. It is an outcome to which explicit commitments should be made by the organization and the consultant at the outset of the consultant's work.

An example illustrates the importance of this point. Suppose that a consultant is hired to design and implement an incentive payment program. What might he or she do for the firm? First, the consultant might identify jobs that lend themselves to an incentive system. Next, seminars on the proposed type of incentive plan might be conducted by the consultant for managers, supervisors, and their employees. A program of job study might come next, in which standards of one kind or another would be determined by the consultant.

This list of activities could be expanded and completed, but there is little point in doing so, for I think that it describes a relatively unproductive use of consulting services. If managers are to learn how to make effective use of incentive payment throughout the organization, they must learn to perform these activities on their own. The consultant may need to teach the managers how to identify jobs that are amenable to the plan so that they can perform this activity without further help from the consultant. Next, the consultant might help the managers develop and present a series of seminars on the incentive plan for supervisors. The supervisors, in turn, might learn to conduct discussion sessions for their employees in which the incentive plan is explored. Following this, plant personnel who have been trained by the consultant might execute a program of job study, and so on.

The main point to consider when investing in consulting is that the value of the consultant must be comparable to any other investment—such as equipment purchases. We would not invest in word-processing equipment without ensuring that training is available to equip members of the organization to use this equipment, but we often fail to realize that when we invest in expert advice we must also make sure that personnel are trained to use this advice in some productive way. This failure may account for much of management's failure to make use of the techniques for improving productivity that have been available for decades.

"Things that do not change remain the same."

Suggested
Resources

POSITIVE REINFORCEMENT

Business, Behaviorism, and the Bottom Line. Del Mar, Calif.: CRM Films, ND.

Skinner, B. F. *Beyond Freedom and Dignity.* New York: Alfred A. Knopf, 1971.

Wheeler, H. (ed.), *Beyond The Punitive Society.* San Francisco: W. H. Freeman, 1973.

INCENTIVE SYSTEMS

McCormick, E. J. *Job Analysis: Methods and Applications.* New York: AMACOM, 1979.

Von Kaas, H. K. *Making Wage Incentives Work.* New York: American Management Association, 1971.

SCANLON PLAN

Cummings, T. G., and Molloy, E. S. *Improving Productivity and the Quality of Work Life.* New York: Praeger, 1977.

Lesieur, F. G. (ed.), *The Scanlon Plan—A Frontier in Labor-Management Cooperation.* Cambridge, Mass.: MIT Press, 1968.

JOB ENRICHMENT

Herzberg, F. *The Managerial Choice: to be Efficient and to be Human.* Homewood, Ill.: Dow Jones—Irwin, 1976.

Yorks, L. *Job Enrichment Revisited.* New York: AMACOM, 1979.

MANAGEMENT BY OBJECTIVES

McConkey, D. D. *How to Manage by Results.* New York: AMACOM, 1976.

Raia, A. P. *Managing by Objectives.* Glenview, Ill.: Scott Foresman, 1974.

SYSTEM FOUR AND SURVEY FEEDBACK

Likert, R., and Likert, J. G. *New Ways of Managing Conflict.* New York: McGraw-Hill, 1976.

Wieland, G. F., and Lee, H. *Changing Hospitals.* London: Tavistock, 1971.

PUBLISHERS' ADDRESSES

AMACOM, 135 West 50th Street, New York, N.Y. 10020

American Management Association, New York, N.Y. 10020

CRM Films, 110 Fifteenth St., Del Mar, CA 92104

Dow Jones-Irwin, 1818 Ridge Rd., Homewood, IL 60430

Freeman, Cooper, & Co., 1736 Stockton St., San Francisco, CA 94133

Alfred A. Knopf, Inc., 400 Hahn Rd., Westminster, MD 21157

McGraw-Hill Book Co., 1221 Avenue of the Americas, New York, N.Y. 10020

MIT Press, 28 Carleton St., Cambridge, MA 02142

Praeger Pubs., 383 Madison Ave., New York, N.Y. 10017

Scott Foresman & Co., 1900 E. Lake Drive, Glenview, IL 60025

Tavistock Publications, Ltd., 11 New Fetter Land, London EC4 England

Index

To order any of these books, please complete the form below.

DO IT NOW: How To Stop Procrastinating, Dr. William Knaus. In DO IT NOW, the author explains how you can stop putting things off by breaking the procrastination habit. Dr. Knaus shows how to recognize and overcome the bad habits that cause you to delay and postpone. Included are simple techniques for stimulating a person into action.

$5.95   paperback (216606) $11.95   hardback (216614)

QUALITY CIRCLES MASTER GUIDE: Increasing Productivity with People Power, Sud Ingle. This book shows exactly how the productivity techniques used so effectively in Japan can be applied to Western technology to improve performance and productivity on the job. This guide explains step-by-step the methods used to create a harmonious feeling among workers, improve morale, produce higher quality products without increasing costs, and get started on a quality drive without having to make a large investment. A must book for managers.

$14.95   paperback (745000) $24.95   hardback (745018)

THINK ON YOUR FEET: The Art of Thinking and Speaking Under Pressure, Kenneth Wydro. For anyone who must speak in front of a large group of people here's a book that reveals dozens of exercises, examples and insights into the creative process of quick thinking. THINK ON YOUR FEET shows how to relax and free the creative mind instantly, how to take command of any situation, how to develop confidence, and much, much more.

$4.95   paperback (917807) $11.95   hardback (917815)

You can obtain these and other fine Spectrum Books at your local bookstore or you can use the order form below.